World War II:
Core Documents

World War II:
Core Documents

Selected and Introduced by

Jennifer D. Keene

Ashbrook Press

© 2018 Ashbrook Center, Ashland University

Library of Congress Cataloging-in-Publication Data

World War II: Core Documents;
Selected and Introduced by Jennifer D. Keene

p. cm.
Includes Index
1. United States – Politics and government.

ISBN 978-1-878802-35-4

(pbk.)

Cover Images, above the title, left to right:
President Franklin D. Roosevelt, ca. 1941 (Farm Security Administration/Office of War Information Photograph Collection, Library of Congress, LC-USW33- 042784-ZC).

General Douglas MacArthur in Manilla, Philippines, August 24, 1945 (Library of Congress, LC-USZ62-21027).

Ansel Adams, "Portrait of Michael Yonimitsu, X-Ray Specialist, Manzanar Relocation Center, California," 1943 (Library of Congress, LC-DIG-ppprs-00254).

"WAC – This Is My War Too," 1941– 1945 (World War II Posters, National Archives and Records Administration, 515988).

John Bottega, "A. Philip Randolph," 1963, for World Telegram and Sun (Library of Congress, LC-USZ62-119495).

Cover Image, below the title:
"General Dwight D. Eisenhower gives the order of the day, 'Full victory—nothing else,' to paratroopers somewhere in England, just before they board their airplanes to participate in the invasion of the continent of Europe," June 6, 1944. (Library of Congress, LC-USZ62-25600).

Ashbrook Center at Ashland University
401 College Avenue
Ashland, Ohio 44805
www.Ashbrook.org

About the Ashbrook Center

The Ashbrook Center restores and strengthens the capacities of the American people for constitutional self-government. Ashbrook teaches students and teachers across our country what America is and what she represents in the long history of the world. Offering a variety of resources and programs, Ashbrook is the largest university-based educator in the enduring principles and practice of free government. Dedicated in 1983 by President Ronald Reagan, the Ashbrook Center is governed by its own board and responsible for raising all of the funds necessary for its many programs.

Visit us online at Ashbrook.org, TeachingAmericanHistory.org, and 50coredocs.org.

Contents

General Editor's Introduction..i

Introduction..iii

1. Neutrality Act of 1935 (August 31, 1935) 1

2. Bennett Champ Clark, A Senator Defends the First Neutrality Act (December 1935).. 4

3. Franklin D. Roosevelt, President Roosevelt Defends Lend-Lease (December 17, 1940) 10

4. Franklin D. Roosevelt, "Arsenal of Democracy" Fireside Chat (December 29, 1940) 14

5. Franklin D. Roosevelt, "The Four Freedoms" (January 6, 1941) 22

6. Gallup Polls (January 1940 – January 1941).............................. 27

7. Eleanor Roosevelt, The First Lady Visits Tuskegee (April 1, 1941) 44

8. Charles Lindbergh, "America First" (April 23, 1941) 46

9. Franklin D. Roosevelt, Executive Order 8802 – Prohibition of Discrimination in the Defense Industry (June 25, 1941) 51

10. The Atlantic Charter (August 14, 1941)................................... 53

11. Franklin D. Roosevelt, Fireside Chat on the *Greer* Incident (September 11, 1941).. 55

12. Robert A. Taft, "Repeal of Neutrality Act Means War" (October 28, 1941) 62

13. Gallup Polls (April - October 1941) 65

14. Claude R. Wickard, Reacting to Pearl Harbor (December 7, 1941) 75

15. Franklin D. Roosevelt, "A Date Which Will Live in Infamy" (December 8, 1941)... 87

16. Franklin D. Roosevelt, Executive Order No. 9066 – Resulting in the Relocation of Japanese (February 19, 1942) 89

17. Japanese American Evacuation (April – May 1942) 92

18. First News of the Final Solution (August 10 – 11, 1942) 93

19. James J. Fahey, *Pacific War Diary* (1942 – 1945) 96

20. A. Philip Randolph, "Why Should We March?" (November 1942) 106

21. Franklin D. Roosevelt, Executive Order 9346 – Establishing a Committee on Fair Employment Practice (May 27, 1943) 111

22. United States Army Women's Auxilary Corps, Questions and Answers About the WAAC (1943) 114

23. Ernie Pyle, "The Death of Captain Waskow" (January 10, 1944) 121

24. Corporal Rupert Trimmingham's Letters to *Yank* Magazine (April 28, 1944 and July 28, 1944) 124

25. Dwight D. Eisenhower, D-Day Statement to the Allied Expeditionary Force (June 5 – 6, 1944) 126

26. Stopping the Holocaust (August 9 and 14, 1944) 129

27. Ansel Adams, Manzanar: Excerpt from *Born Free and Equal* (1944) 132

28. General Douglas MacArthur, Radio Address Upon Returning to the Philippines (October 20, 1944) 135

29. *Korematsu v. US* (December 18, 1944) 137

30. G.I. Roundtable Series, "Do You Want Your Wife to Work After the War?" (1944) 145

31. Potsdam Declaration (July 26, 1945) 150

32. Harry S. Truman, Press Release Alerting the Nation About the Atomic Bomb (August 6, 1945) 153

33. United States Strategic Bombing Survey, *The Effects of Atomic Bombs on Hiroshima and Nagasaki* (July 1, 1946) 157

34. Justice Robert H. Jackson, *Report on the Nuremberg Trials* (October 7, 1946) 162

Appendices 167
Appendix A: Thematic Table of Contents 169
Appendix B: Study Questions 172
Appendix C: Suggestions For Further Reading 182

General Editor's Introduction

This collection of documents on World War II is the third volume in an extended series of document collections from the Ashbrook Center that will cover major periods, themes, and institutions in American history and government. This volume begins its story – focused on the experience of the war in America, but not neglecting the experience of Americans who fought – in 1935, as Americans expressed their wariness of involvement in another European war by passing a neutrality act. It recounts the debate over neutrality as conflict approached and then overwhelmed Europe. All such debate ended with the Japanese attack on Pearl Harbor in 1941, but new issues arose as the war churned on, including internment of Japanese Americans; the treatment of African-Americans in the United States and in its Armed Forces; the role of women in the war effort and how this might change their lives after the war; and the principles that should shape the post-war world. These issues and the two events with which the collection ends – the Nuremberg trials and the atomic bombing of Hiroshima and Nagasaki – foreshadow the world the war helped bring about.

When the series of Ashbrook document collections is complete, it will be comprehensive, and also authoritative, because it will present America's story in the words of those who wrote it – America's presidents, labor leaders, farmers, philosophers, industrialists, politicians, workers, explorers, religious leaders, judges, soldiers; its slaveholders and abolitionists; its expansionists and isolationists; its reformers and stand-patters; its strict and broad constructionists; its hard-eyed realists and visionary utopians – all united in their commitment to equality and liberty, yet all also divided often by their different understandings of these most fundamental American ideas. The documents are about all this – the still unfinished American experiment with self-government.

As this volume does, each of the volumes in the series will contain key documents on its period, theme, or institution, selected by an expert and reviewed by an editorial board. Each volume will have an introduction highlighting key documents and themes. In an appendix to each volume, there will also be a thematic table of contents, showing the connections between various documents. Another appendix will provide study questions for each document, as well as questions that refer to other documents in the collection, tying them together as the thematic table of contents does. Each document will be checked against an authoritative original source and have an introduction outlining its significance. We will provide notes to each document to identify people, events, movements, or ideas that may be unfamiliar to non-specialist readers and to improve understanding of the document's historical context.

In sum, our intent is that the documents and their supporting material provide reliable and unique access to the richness of the American story.

Jennifer D. Keene, Professor of History, Chapman University, selected the documents and wrote the introductions. Ellen Tucker and David Tucker edited the collection, with the assistance of Josh Distel. Lisa Ormiston of the Ashbrook Center oversaw production. This volume was made possible by the generous support of Dick Uihlein, Uline and other Ashbrook donors.

David Tucker
Senior Fellow
Ashbrook Center

Introduction

At 6 am on December 7, 1941, two consecutive waves of Japanese bombers, torpedo planes, and dive-bombers attacked the Pearl Harbor naval station on the Hawaiian island of Oahu. The attack on Pearl Harbor was part of a coordinated Japanese assault throughout the Pacific that also targeted the Philippines, Guam, and Hong Kong (Document 14). The United States declared war against Japan the next day. "There is no blinking at the fact that our people, our territory, and our interests are in grave danger," President Franklin D. Roosevelt (FDR) told the nation (Document 15). Four days later Germany and Italy declared war on the United States. The nation was now at war on two fronts, fighting determined and capable enemies.

The attack on Pearl Harbor was the culmination of a decade of tension between Japan and the United States. President Roosevelt tried to use a series of escalating sanctions to curtail Japan's ambitions to extend its territorial control throughout Asia. Western nations, including the United States, had little interest in ceding their colonies or overseas markets to Japan. In the end, Japan elected to push out Western imperial nations by force.

The Japanese attack unified the nation, ending two years of debate over whether or not the wars in Europe and the Pacific were America's wars to fight. Most pre-war discussion, however, had focused on how to respond to German, not Japanese, aggression. The prevailing feeling that it had been a mistake to get involved in World War I led to the adoption of a strict policy of neutrality in the 1930s (Documents 1 and 2). After Hitler's 1939 attack on Poland ignited World War II, Roosevelt struggled to reconcile the nation's desire to help Great Britain defeat Nazi Germany with the policy of official neutrality (Document 6). FDR endorsed sending economic aid to Great Britain as the best way to stay out of the war, arguing that without this American lifeline Great Britain would succumb to Nazi Germany (Documents 3 and 4). Charles Lindbergh, the most prominent member of the America First movement, openly challenged FDR's claim that Nazi Germany posed a direct threat to the United States (Document 8). These criticisms forced FDR to proceed cautiously, even as he aligned the United States more closely ideologically (Documents 5 and 10) and militarily (Document 11) with Great Britain. By the fall of 1941, the majority of Americans supported FDR's decision to shoot on sight German submarines trying to sink British merchant ships transporting American goods (Document 13). Critics continued to attack FDR's gradual abandonment of neutrality (Document 12), but Pearl Harbor ended all debate.

Even before the declarations of war, American society was changing as a result of overseas conflicts. A peacetime draft was introduced in 1940, and the exploding war trade pulled migrants to major cities in search of well-paying jobs. Both developments concerned African Americans who worried that racial discrimination would prevent them from having equal opportunities in the military and defense industries. FDR managed to halt a threatened March on Washington by promising access to high-paying defense jobs (Document 9), while First Lady Eleanor Roosevelt offered more adamant support for racial equality by supporting the training of black military pilots (Document 7). Throughout the war African Americans challenged segregation in the military and on the home front, racial discrimination in the workplace and housing market, and the seating of German POWs in restaurants while black soldiers were turned away (Documents 20, 21, and 24).

Eager for explanations after the attack on Pearl Harbor, some Americans suspected that Hawaiian residents of Japanese ancestry must have helped Japan. Prejudice against Asian Americans was not new, but the war amplified fears that Japanese immigrants and Japanese Americans were disloyal. In the winter of 1942, FDR authorized their exclusion from the West Coast, and soon the War Relocation Authority was overseeing the removal of 120,000 people of Japanese ancestry to internment camps (Documents 16 and 17). Once in the camps, Japanese immigrants and Japanese Americans struggled to retain a semblance of normal life, and photographs offer some insight into their experiences (Document 27). Legal challenges to the Japanese internment reached the Supreme Court, which in 1944 upheld the constitutionality of the removal process without ruling directly on the constitutionality of internment in *Korematsu v. US* (Document 29).

In writing the majority decision for *Korematsu*, Justice Hugo Black noted that "we deem it unjustifiable" to call the internment camps "concentration camps with all the ugly connotations that term implies." His remark revealed that by 1944, Americans were well aware of Adolph Hitler's plan to exterminate European Jews. The first news of the Final Solution reached Washington, D.C. in 1942, shortly after the German decision to initiate a systematic genocide to replace uncoordinated mass killings (Document 18). By 1944, American bombers were in range of the Auschwitz extermination camp in Poland but the military decided against bombing the gas chambers and crematorium, a decision that proved controversial (Document 26). Instead, after Germany surrendered on May 7, 1945 the United States took the lead in organizing the postwar Nuremburg Trials to punish Nazi perpetrators for crimes against humanity (Document 34).

Of course, before it could try enemy leaders in Germany (and also Japan) for war crimes, the United States and its allies had to win victory on both fronts. Mobilizing the nation's manpower meant recruiting men and women to serve the war effort in a multitude of ways. Eventually, over 16 million men served in the armed forces, a figure that included 10 million draftees. The military suffered approximately 291,000 deaths and 670,000 wounded. Almost 350,000 women served in the armed forces, including 150,000 women in the Women's Army Corps who served as radio operators, clerks, technicians, and auto mechanics (Document 22). Three million civilian women joined the 16 million already in the workforce, the highest number of paid female workers yet recorded. Would these experiences working in civilian factories or serving in uniform permanently change the role of women in society? This question was anticipated and discussed even before the war was officially over (Document 30).

For men on the front lines, in Europe and in the Pacific, victory came with a high cost. Nearly two-thirds of the men who died in combat were killed in 1944 and 1945. The closer the Allies got to defeating Japan and Germany, the harder these enemy armies fought. The wartime diary of James J. Fahey and dispatches by war correspondent Ernie Pyle reveal the emotional and psychological side of combat (Documents 19 and 23). The differing leadership styles of General Dwight D. Eisenhower in Europe and General Douglas MacArthur in the Pacific offer a study in contrasts, yet each proved inspiring to the men under their command (Documents 25 and 28).

President Franklin D. Roosevelt did not live to see the end of the war. When he died of a cerebral hemorrhage on April 12, 1945, Harry S. Truman became president. He soon learned of a four-year secret weapons program called the Manhattan Project that was attempting to produce an atomic bomb. In July, the United States successfully tested its first atomic bomb in the New Mexico desert. Upon hearing the news, Truman issued a veiled ultimatum to Japan to immediately surrender or suffer immense destruction (Document 31). On August 6, 1945 the United States dropped an atomic bomb on Hiroshima, Japan, killing 80,000 people. "I shall give further consideration and make further recommendations to the Congress as to how atomic power can become a powerful and forceful influence towards the maintenance of world peace," Truman told the American people while announcing the attack

(Document 32). Three days later, a second nuclear bomb dropped on Nagasaki killed 35,000 people. Japan surrendered on August 14, 1945.

Victory on the battlefield against Japan and Germany did not bring certainty that years of peace would follow. Amid the celebrations, a host of new anxieties arose. What would the existence of atomic bombs mean for the future? US investigators offered one answer when they insisted that surveying the devastation in Hiroshima and Nagasaki would help Americans devise ways to defend their cities from similar attacks (Document 33). World War II was over, but the nuclear age had begun.

World War II:
Core Documents

Document 1

Neutrality Act of 1935
August 31, 1935

In response to rising tensions in the world, Congress passed the Neutrality Act of 1935 to prevent the United States from becoming embroiled in future wars. These restrictions reflected the general American view in the 1930s that trading with warring nations from 1914 - 1917 had caused the United States to enter World War I. President Franklin D. Roosevelt invoked the act in October after Italy invaded Ethiopia. Congress expanded upon these restrictions in 1936 by prohibiting loans to belligerent nations. In 1937, Congress mandated that nations at war could only purchase goods from the US that were not war-related and had to transport them in their own ships, a policy known as "cash and carry." These restrictions limited American involvement in the Spanish Civil War (1936–39), which pitted right-wing nationalists, supported by Germany, against left-wing republicans, supported by the Soviet Union.

Source: U.S. Department of State, Publication 1983, Peace and War: United States Foreign Policy, 1931 - 1941 *(Washington, D.C.: U.S. Government Printing Office, 1943), p. 265 - 271. https://goo.gl/vGzRCg*

. . . Resolved by the Senate and House of Representatives of the United States of America in Congress assembled, That upon the outbreak or during the progress of war between, or among, two or more foreign states, the President shall proclaim such fact, and it shall thereafter be unlawful to export arms, ammunition, or implements of war from any place in the United States, or possessions of the United States, to any port of such belligerent states, or to any neutral port for transshipment to, or for the use of, a belligerent country.

The President, by proclamation, shall definitely enumerate the arms, ammunition, or implements of war, the export of which is prohibited by this Act.

The President may, from time to time, by proclamation, extend such embargo upon the export of arms, ammunition, or implements of war to other states as and when they may become involved in such war.

Whoever, in violation of any of the provisions of this section, shall export, or attempt to export, or cause to be exported, arms, ammunition, or implements of war from the United States, or any of its possessions, shall be fined not more than $10,000 or imprisoned not more than five years, or both, and the property, vessel, or vehicle containing the same shall be subject to the provisions of sections 1 to 8, inclusive, title 6, chapter 30, of the Act approved June 15, 1917 (40 Stat. 223-225; U. S. C., title 22, sess. 238-245).

. . . SEC. 5. Whenever, during any war in which the United States is neutral, the President shall find that special restrictions placed on the use of the ports and territorial waters of the United States, or of its possessions, by the submarines of a foreign nation will serve to maintain peace between the United States and foreign nations, or to protect the commercial interests of the United States and its citizens, or to promote the security of the United States, and shall make proclamation thereof, it shall thereafter be unlawful for any such submarine to enter a port or the territorial waters of the United States or any of its possessions, or to depart therefrom, except under such conditions and subject to such limitations as the President may prescribe. When, in his judgment, the conditions which have caused him to issue his proclamation have ceased to exist, he shall revoke his proclamation and the provisions of this section shall thereupon cease to apply.

SEC. 6. Whenever, during any war in which the United States is neutral, the President shall find that the maintenance of peace between the United States and foreign nations, or the protection of the lives of citizens of the United States, or the protection of the commercial interests of the United States and its citizens, or the security of the United States requires that the American citizens should refrain from traveling as passengers on the vessels of any belligerent nation, he shall so proclaim, and thereafter no citizen of the United States shall travel on any vessel of any belligerent nation except at his own risk, unless in accordance with such rules and regulations as the President shall prescribe: Provided, however, That the provisions of this section shall not apply to a citizen travelling on the vessel of a belligerent whose voyage was begun in advance of the date of the President's proclamation, and who had no opportunity to discontinue his voyage after that date: And provided further, That they shall not apply under ninety days after the date of the President's proclamation to a citizen returning from a foreign country to the United States or to any of its possessions. When, in the President's judgment, the conditions which have caused him to issue his proclamation have ceased to exist, he shall revoke his proclamation and the provisions of this section shall thereupon cease to apply.

SEC. 7. In every case of the violation of any of the provisions of this Act where a specific penalty is not herein provided, such violator or violators, upon conviction, shall be fined not more than $10,000 or imprisoned not more than five years, or both. . . .

Document 2

A Senator Defends the First Neutrality Act

Senator Bennett Champ Clark
December 1935

Senator Bennett Champ Clark (1890–1954, D-MO), who served in the U.S. Senate from 1933 to 1945, was a strong proponent of making neutrality a cornerstone of American foreign policy. He made his case directly to the public in this December 1935 Harper's Monthly article, "Detour Around War: A Proposal for a New American Policy." Clark served on the Senate's Munitions Investigation Committee, popularly known as the Nye Committee for its chairman, Senator Gerald P. Nye (R-ND). In the mid-1930s the Nye Committee held a series of investigations into "Merchants of Death" conspiracy theories but uncovered little hard evidence. Nonetheless, the belief persisted that munitions manufacturers and financiers had secretly maneuvered the United States into WWI to continue their profitable war trade and to secure repayment of war loans to the Allies. In this opinion piece, Clark urges a renewal and expansion of the 1935 Neutrality Act. Congress heeded his call by renewing the act and adding a prohibition on loans to warring nations in the Neutrality Law of 1936. In 1937, Congress mandated that nations at war could purchase from the US only goods that were not war-related and must transport them in their own ships, a policy known as "cash and carry."

Source: Bennett Champ Clark, "Detour Around War: A Proposal for a New American Policy," Harper's Monthly, December 1935, 1–9.

. . . At the present the desire to keep the United States from becoming involved in any war between foreign nations seems practically unanimous among the rank and file of American citizens; but it must be remembered there was an almost equally strong demand to keep us out of the last war. In August, 1914, few could have conceived that America would be dragged into a European conflict in which we had no original part and the ramifications of which we did not even understand. Even as late as November, 1916, President

Wilson was reelected because he "kept us out of war." Yet five months later we were fighting to "save the world for democracy" in the "war to end war."

In the light of that experience, and in the red glow of war fires burning in the old countries, it is high time we gave some thought to the hard, practical question of just how we propose to stay out of present and future international conflicts. No one who has made an honest attempt to face the issue will assert that there is an easy answer. But if we have learned anything at all, we know the inevitable and tragic end to a policy of drifting and trusting to luck. We know that however strong is the will of the American people to refrain from mixing in other people's quarrels, that will can be made effective only if we have a sound, definite policy from the beginning.

Such a policy must be built upon a program to safeguard our neutrality. No lesson of the World War is more clear than that such a policy cannot be improvised after war breaks out. It must be determined in advance, before it is too late to apply reason. I contend with all possible earnestness that if we want to avoid being drawn into this war now forming, or any other future war, we must formulate a definite, workable policy of neutral relations with belligerent nations.

Some of us in the Senate, particularly the members of the Munitions Investigation Committee, have delved rather deeply into the matter of how the United States has been drawn into past wars, and what forces are at work to frighten us again into the traps set by Mars. As a result of these studies, Senator Nye and I introduced the three proposals for neutrality legislation which were debated so vigorously in the last session of the Congress. A part of that legislative program was battered through both houses in the closing hours of the session late in August; a very vital part of it was held in abeyance.

Senator Nye and I made no claims then, and make none now, that the neutrality proposals will provide an absolute and infallible guarantee against our involvement in war. But we do believe that the United States can stay out of war if it wants to, and if its citizens understand what is necessary to preserve our neutrality. We feel that the temporary legislation already passed and the legislation we shall vigorously push at the coming session of the Congress point the only practical way....

The act is to terminate February 29, 1936. It is a stop-gap only. But it is pointing the way we intend to go.

The President is empowered to enumerate definitely the arms, munitions, and implements of war, the exportation of which is prohibited by this act. On September 27th President Roosevelt made this enumeration in a proclamation, following closely the list submitted to the disarmament conference at Geneva in our government's proposals for international control of the munitions industry. A National Munitions Control Board has been established, composed of the Secretaries of State, Treasury, War, Navy, and Commerce, with the administration of the board in the Department of State. It is contemplated that by November 29th, when the Act takes effect, the manufacturers and exporters of war implements will all be listed in the office of this board. After that date such materials as are specified may not be exported without a license issued by the board to cover such shipment. This will, obviously, permit the government to prohibit shipments to belligerent nations. The act makes it unlawful for any American vessel to "carry arms, ammunition, or implements of war to any port of the belligerent countries named in such proclamation as being at war, or to any neutral port for transshipment to, or for use in, a belligerent country."

Further provisions of the act empower the President to restrict the use of American ports and waters to submarines of foreign nations in the event such use might disturb our position of neutrality, and to proclaim the conditions under which American citizens on belligerent ships during war must travel entirely at their own risk.

Two provisions from our original program failed to pass: prohibition of loans and credits to belligerent nations, and the application of strict embargoes upon contraband materials other than munitions and war implements....

I have called the present neutrality act a stop-gap. But it has not stopped the activities of our American war-munitions makers anxious for profits from imminent conflicts. Reports from centers of manufacturing and exporting of war implements all tell the same story: there is a boom in war preparations. Chambers of commerce in cities with large war-materials plants proudly report reemployment of skilled munitions makers in large numbers, the stepping up of output to as high as three hundred per cent, the rushing to completion of new additions to plants. Day-and-night shifts in the brass and copper mills, rising prices and large shipments of these metals, and the acquisition of large capital for immediate wartime scale production, all indicate that Mars has waved his magic wand in our direction.

Where are these war-implements shipments going? There is no proof that the munitions makers are trying to "beat the embargo" which will prohibit shipments to belligerents after November 29th, but it stands to reason they are making hay while the sun shines. Our Munitions Investigation Committee has not had time to look into immediate developments, but it needs no stretch of imagination to contemplate the rich profits that would flow from an Italian-

Ethiopian war,[1] with England jumping into the fray against Italy, and other European nations following suit on one side or the other.

And, of course, there's lots of war business right here at home. We have increased our expenditures on our Army and Navy in preparation for another and more dreadful war more rapidly than any European country in the period since the World War. . . .

When the Congress meets in January, facing the expiration of the neutrality act on February 29th, the battle for a practical policy of neutrality will have to be fought all over again. We who believe that the detour around another devastating war is to be found only in new conceptions of neutrality will fight for the retention of the present legislation and for the passage of the two items left out in the cold at the adjournment of the Congress.

[I firmly believe, whatever the status of the Italo-Ethiopian dispute at that time, whatever the position of other European powers as belligerents or as neutrals, that the United States of America cannot turn back to a policy of so-called neutrality that finally pulls us into conflict with one or all the belligerents. Surely it is obvious that the legislation forcing mandatory embargoes upon war materials will serve to check the growth of another vast munitions trade with warring powers and the dangers that follow a swing of our foreign trade in favor of our munitions customers and against those who cannot purchase the munitions. Why shall we contend for embargoes upon contraband articles as well, and prohibition of loans and credits to belligerents? Because it takes these two items to complete any sort of workable neutrality program. If we are in earnest about neutrality we may as well plan to be neutral. . . .]

[Let us foresee that under conditions of modern warfare everything supplied to the enemy population has the same effect as supplies to the enemy army, and will become contraband. Food, clothing, lumber, leather, chemicals – everything, in fact, with the possible exception of sporting goods and luxuries (and these aid in maintaining civilian "morale") – are as important aids to winning the war as are munitions] Let us foresee also that our ships carrying contraband will be seized, bombed from the air or sunk by submarines. Let us not claim as a right what is an impossibility. The only way we can maintain our neutral rights is to fight the whole world. If we are not prepared to do that we

---

[1] The Second Italo-Ethiopian war had begun when Italian forces invaded Ethiopia from Italian Somaliland in October 1935. The English and French would not move to stop the Italian incursion into Ethiopia, fearing that doing so would push Italy into alliance with Germany.

can only pretend to enforce our rights against one side, and go to war to defend them against the other side. We might at least abandon pretense.

On the matter of loans and credits to belligerents, the train of events which pulled us into the World War is equally significant. Correspondence which our Munitions Investigation Committee discovered in the files of the State Department offers illuminating proof that there can be no true neutrality when our nation is allowed to finance one side of a foreign war. [One letter, written by Secretary Robert Lansing to President Wilson, dated September 5, 1915, lucidly points out that loans for the Allies were absolutely necessary to enable them to pay for the tremendous trade in munitions, war materials generally, food stuffs, and the like, or else that trade would have to stop. He declared that the Administration's "true spirit of neutrality" must not stand in the way of the demands of commerce. About one month later the first great loan – the Anglo-French loan of $500,000,000 – was floated by a syndicate headed by J. P. Morgan and Company. This company had been the purchasing agents for Allied supplies in the United States since early in 1915. Other loans to the Allied powers quickly followed....]

"But, think of the profits!" cry our theorists. "America will never give up her lucrative trade in munitions and necessities of life when war starts!"...

Just who profited from the last war? Labor got some of the crumbs in the form of high wages and steady jobs. But where is labor to-day with its fourteen million unemployed? Agriculture received high prices for its products during the period of the War and has been paying the price of that brief inflation in the worst and longest agricultural depression in all history. Industry made billions in furnishing the necessities of war to the belligerents and then suffered terrific re-action like the dope addict's morning after. War and depression – ugly, misshapen inseparable twins – must be considered together. Each is a catapult for the other. The present world-wide depression is a direct result of the World War. Every war in modern history has been followed by a major depression.

Therefore I say, let the man seeking profits from war or the war-torn countries do so at his own risk....

[If there are those so brave as to risk getting us into war by traveling in the war zones – if there are those so valiant that they do not care how many people are killed as a result of their traveling, let us tell them, and let us tell the world that from now on their deaths will be a misfortune to their own families alone, not to the whole nation.]

The profiteers and others who oppose any rational neutrality shout: "You would sacrifice our national honor!" Some declare we are about to haul down the American flag, and in a future war the belligerents will trample on our rights and treat us with contempt. Some of these arguments are trundled out by our naval bureaucracy. The admirals, I am told, objected strenuously when the State Department suggested a new policy of neutrality somewhat along these lines.

I deny with every fiber of my being that our national honor demands that we must sacrifice the flower of our youth to safeguard the profits of a privileged few. I deny that it is necessary to turn back the hands of civilization to maintain our national honor. I repudiate any such definition of honor. Is it not time for every lover of our country to do the same thing?

Document 3

President Roosevelt Defends Lend-Lease
Franklin D. Roosevelt
December 17, 1940

When World War II began in 1939, President Roosevelt tried and failed to get a complete repeal of the Neutrality Laws. Instead, Congress passed the 1939 Neutrality Law that allowed trade with warring nations on a "cash and carry" basis (nations at war were permitted only to purchase non-war related goods and had to transport them in their own ships). The new law, however, retained the ban on war loans to warring nations. By 1940, this provision threatened to shut down trade with Britain, which now needed credit to continue buying munitions, raw materials, and food from the United States. In response, Roosevelt devised Lend-Lease. In this December 17, 1940 press conference, Roosevelt described how this program would work and defended it as consistent with the Neutrality Law. Congress passed the Lend-Lease Act in March 1941.

Source: Franklin D. Roosevelt: "Press Conference," December 17, 1940. Online by Gerhard Peters and John T. Woolley, The American Presidency Project. https://goo.gl/U33U33

The President: . . . In the present world situation of course there is absolutely no doubt in the mind of a very overwhelming number of Americans that the best immediate defense of the United States is the success of Great Britain in defending itself; and that, therefore, quite aside from our historic and current interest in the survival of democracy, in the world as a whole, it is equally important from a selfish point of view of American defense, that we should do everything to help the British Empire to defend itself. . . .

I remember 1914 very well, and I will give you an illustration: In 1914 I was up at Eastport, Maine, with the family the end of July, and I got a telegram from the Navy Department that it looked as if war would break out in Europe the next day. Actually it did break out in a few hours, when Germany invaded Belgium. So I went across from the island and took a train down to Ellsworth, where I got on the Bar Harbor Express. I went into the smoking room. The smoking room of the Express was filled with gentlemen from banking and brokerage offices in New York, most of whom were old friends of mine; and they began giving me their opinion about the impending world war in Europe. These eminent bankers and brokers assured me, and made it good with bets, that there wasn't enough money in all the world to carry on a European war for more than three months – bets at even money; that the bankers would stop the war within six months – odds of 2 to 1; that it was humanly impossible – physically impossible – for a European war to last for six months – odds of 4 to 1; and so forth and so on. Well, actually, I suppose I must have won those – they were small, five-dollar bets – I must have made a hundred dollars. I wish I had bet a lot more.

There was the best economic opinion in the world that the continuance of war was absolutely dependent on money in the bank. Well, you know what happened....

Orders from Great Britain are therefore a tremendous asset to American national defense; because they automatically create additional facilities. I am talking selfishly, from the American point of view – nothing else. Therefore, from the selfish point of view, that production must be encouraged by us. There are several ways of encouraging it – not just one, as the narrow-minded fellow I have been talking about might assume, and has assumed. He has assumed that the only way was to repeal certain existing statutes, like the Neutrality Act [Document 1] and the old Johnson Act[1] and a few other things like that; and then to lend the money to Great Britain to be spent over here – either lend it through private banking circles, as was done in the earlier days of the previous war, or make it a loan from this Government to the British Government.

Well, that is one type of mind that can think only of that method[, which is] somewhat banal.

There is another one which is also somewhat banal – we may come to it, I don't know – and that is a gift; in other words, for us to pay for all these munitions, ships, plants, guns, et cetera, and make a gift of them to Great Britain. I am not at all sure that that is a necessity, and I am not at all sure that Great Britain would care to have a gift from the taxpayers of the United States. I doubt it very much.

Well, there are other possible ways, and those ways are being explored. All I can do is to speak in very general terms, because we are in the middle of it. I

---

[1] The 1934 Johnson Act prohibited nations in default on their World War I war loan repayments from marketing their bonds in the United States.

have been at it now three or four weeks, exploring other methods of continuing the building up of our productive facilities and continuing automatically the flow of munitions to Great Britain. I will just put it this way, not as an exclusive alternative method, but as one of several other possible methods that might be devised toward that end.

It is possible – I will put it that way – for the United States to take over British orders, and, because they are essentially the same kind of munitions that we use ourselves, turn them into American orders. We have enough money to do it. And thereupon, as to such portion of them as the military events of the future determine to be right and proper for us to allow to go to the other side, either lease or sell the materials, subject to mortgage, to the people on the other side. That would be on the general theory that it may still prove true that the best defense of Great Britain is the best defense of the United States, and therefore that these materials would be more useful to the defense of the United States if they were used in Great Britain, than if they were kept in storage here.

Now, what I am trying to do is to eliminate the dollar sign. That is something brand new in the thoughts of practically everybody in this room, I think – get rid of the silly, foolish old dollar sign.

Well, let me give you an illustration: Suppose my neighbor's home catches fire, and I have a length of garden hose four or five hundred feet away. If he can take my garden hose and connect it up with his hydrant, I may help him to put out his fire. Now, what do I do? I don't say to him before that operation, "Neighbor, my garden hose cost me $15; you have to pay me $15 for it." What is the transaction that goes on? I don't want $15 – I want my garden hose back after the fire is over. All right. If it goes through the fire all right, intact, without any damage to it, he gives it back to me and thanks me very much for the use of it. But suppose it gets smashed up – holes in it – during the fire; we don't have to have too much formality about it, but I say to him, "I was glad to lend you that hose; I see I can't use it any more, it's all smashed up." He says, "How many feet of it were there?" I tell him, "There were 150 feet of it." He says, "All right, I will replace it." Now, if I get a nice garden hose back, I am in pretty good shape.

In other words, if you lend certain munitions and get the munitions back at the end of the war, if they are intact, haven't been hurt – you are all right; if they have been damaged or have deteriorated or have been lost completely, it seems to me you come out pretty well if you have them replaced by the fellow to whom you have lent them.

I can't go into details; and there is no use asking legal questions about how you would do it, because that is the thing that is now under study; but the thought is that we would take over not all, but a very large number of, future British orders; and when they came off the line, whether they were planes or guns or something else, we would enter into some kind of arrangement for their use by the British on the ground that it was the best thing for American defense, with the understanding that when the show was over, we would get repaid sometime in kind, thereby leaving out the dollar mark in the form of a dollar debt and substituting for it a gentleman's obligation to repay in kind. I think you all get it....

Document 4

"Arsenal of Democracy" Fireside Chat
Franklin D. Roosevelt
December 29, 1940

President Franklin D. Roosevelt's fireside chats were weekly radio addresses to the American people about important issues of the day. In this fireside chat, Roosevelt argued that the United States had to do all it could, short of war, to help Great Britain in a fight it was waging alone against Nazi Germany and its Italian ally. FDR faced the difficult task of conveying the seriousness of the threat to the United States while simultaneously reassuring the public that "[o]ur national policy is not directed toward war. Its sole purpose is to keep war away from our country and our people."

World War II had begun in Europe in 1939 after Germany invaded Poland. By December 1940, German troops occupied France, Belgium, Norway, Denmark, and the Netherlands, and Germany had unleashed a relentless bombing campaign against Britain.

Source: Franklin D. Roosevelt: "Fireside Chat," December 29, 1940. Online by Gerhard Peters and John T. Woolley, The American Presidency Project, https://goo.gl/1tsNRc.

My friends:

This is not a fireside chat on war. It is a talk on national security; because the nub of the whole purpose of your President is to keep you now, and your children later, and your grandchildren much later, out of a last-ditch war for the preservation of American independence and all the things that American independence means to you and to me and to ours....

Never before since Jamestown and Plymouth Rock has our American civilization been in such danger as now.

For, on September 27, 1940, by an agreement signed in Berlin, three powerful nations, two in Europe and one in Asia, joined themselves together in the threat that if the United States of America interfered with or blocked the expansion program of these three nations – a program aimed at world control – they would unite in ultimate action against the United States[1]. . . .

Some of our people like to believe that wars in Europe and in Asia are of no concern to us. But it is a matter of most vital concern to us that European and Asiatic war-makers should not gain control of the oceans which lead to this hemisphere.

One hundred and seventeen years ago the Monroe Doctrine was conceived by our Government as a measure of defense in the face of a threat against this hemisphere by an alliance in Continental Europe. Thereafter, we stood on guard in the Atlantic, with the British as neighbors. There was no treaty. There was no "unwritten agreement."

And yet, there was the feeling, proven correct by history, that we as neighbors could settle any disputes in peaceful fashion. The fact is that during the whole of this time the Western Hemisphere has remained free from aggression from Europe or from Asia.

Does anyone seriously believe that we need to fear attack anywhere in the Americas while a free Britain remains our most powerful naval neighbor in the Atlantic? Does anyone seriously believe, on the other hand, that we could rest easy if the Axis powers were our neighbors there?

If Great Britain goes down, the Axis powers will control the continents of Europe, Asia, Africa, Australasia, and the high seas – and they will be in a position to bring enormous military and naval resources against this hemisphere. It is no exaggeration to say that all of us, in all the Americas, would be living at the point of a gun – a gun loaded with explosive bullets, economic as well as military.

We should enter upon a new and terrible era in which the whole world, our hemisphere included, would be run by threats of brute force. To survive in such a world, we would have to convert ourselves permanently into a militaristic power on the basis of war economy.

Some of us like to believe that even if Great Britain falls, we are still safe, because of the broad expanse of the Atlantic and of the Pacific.

But the width of those oceans is not what it was in the days of clipper ships. At one point between Africa and Brazil the distance is less than from Washington to Denver, Colorado: five hours for the latest type of bomber. And

---

[1] FDR is referring to the Tripartite Agreement, a defensive pact made by Germany, Italy, and Japan to come to the others' defense if they were attacked by the United States.

[margin note: Technology has made the world much smaller.]

at the North end of the Pacific Ocean America and Asia almost touch each other.

Even today we have planes that could fly from the British Isles to New England and back again without refueling. And remember that the range of the modern bomber is ever being increased.

During the past week many people in all parts of the nation have told me what they wanted me to say tonight. Almost all of them expressed a courageous desire to hear the plain truth about the gravity of the situation. One telegram, however, expressed the attitude of the small minority who want to see no evil and hear no evil, even though they know in their hearts that evil exists. That telegram begged me not to tell again of the ease with which our American cities could be bombed by any hostile power which had gained bases in this Western Hemisphere. The gist of that telegram was: "Please, Mr. President, don't frighten us by telling us the facts."

Frankly and definitely there is danger ahead – danger against which we must prepare. But we well know that we cannot escape danger, or the fear of danger, by crawling into bed and pulling the covers over our heads.

[margin note: Germany (Nazis) never keep their word.]

Some nations of Europe were bound by solemn non-intervention pacts with Germany. Other nations were assured by Germany that they need never fear invasion. Non-intervention pact or not, the fact remains that they were attacked, overrun and thrown into the modern form of slavery at an hour's notice, or even without any notice at all. As an exiled leader of one of these nations said to me the other day—"The notice was a minus quantity. It was given to my Government two hours after German troops had poured into my country in a hundred places."

The fate of these nations tells us what it means to live at the point of a Nazi gun.

The Nazis have justified such actions by various pious frauds. One of these frauds is the claim that they are occupying a nation for the purpose of "restoring order." Another is that they are occupying or controlling a nation on the excuse that they are "protecting it" against the aggression of somebody else.

For example, Germany has said that she was occupying Belgium to save the Belgians from the British. Would she then hesitate to say to any South American country, "We are occupying you to protect you from aggression by the United States"?

Belgium today is being used as an invasion base against Britain, now fighting for its life. Any South American country, in Nazi hands, would always constitute a jumping-off place for German attack on any one of the other Republics of this hemisphere.

Analyze for yourselves the future of two other places even nearer to Germany if the Nazis won. Could Ireland hold out? Would Irish freedom be permitted as an amazing pet exception in an unfree world? Or the Islands of the Azores which still fly the flag of Portugal after five centuries? You and I think of Hawaii as an outpost of defense in the Pacific. And yet, the Azores are closer to our shores in the Atlantic than Hawaii is on the other side.

There are those who say that the Axis powers would never have any desire to attack the Western Hemisphere. That is the same dangerous form of wishful thinking which has destroyed the powers of resistance of so many conquered peoples. The plain facts are that the Nazis have proclaimed, time and again, that all other races are their inferiors and therefore subject to their orders. And most important of all, the vast resources and wealth of this American Hemisphere constitute the most tempting loot in all the round world.

Let us no longer blind ourselves to the undeniable fact that the evil forces which have crushed and undermined and corrupted so many others are already within our own gates. Your Government knows much about them and every day is ferreting them out.

Their secret emissaries are active in our own and in neighboring countries. They seek to stir up suspicion and dissension to cause internal strife. They try to turn capital against labor, and vice versa. They try to reawaken long slumbering racial and religious enmities which should have no place in this country. They are active in every group that promotes intolerance. They exploit for their own ends our natural abhorrence of war. These trouble-breeders have but one purpose. It is to divide our people into hostile groups and to destroy our unity and shatter our will to defend ourselves.

There are also American citizens, many of them in high places, who, unwittingly in most cases, are aiding and abetting the work of these agents. I do not charge these American citizens with being foreign agents. But I do charge them with doing exactly the kind of work that the dictators want done in the United States.

Let us no longer blind ourselves to the undeniable fact that the evil forces which have crushed and undermined and corrupted so many others are already within our own gates. Your Government knows much about them and every day is ferreting them out.

Their secret emissaries are active in our own and in neighboring countries. They seek to stir up suspicion and dissension to cause internal strife. They try to turn capital against labor, and vice versa. They try to reawaken long slumbering racial and religious enmities which should have no place in this country. They are active in every group that promotes intolerance. They exploit for their own ends our natural abhorrence of war. These trouble-breeders have but one purpose. It is to divide our people into hostile groups and to destroy our unity and shatter our will to defend ourselves.

There are also American citizens, many of them in high places, who, unwittingly in most cases, are aiding and abetting the work of these agents. I do not charge these American citizens with being foreign agents. But I do charge them with doing exactly the kind of work that the dictators want done in the United States.

These people [the "America First" movement][2] not only believe that we can save our own skins by shutting our eyes to the fate of other nations. Some of them go much further than that. They say that we can and should become the friends and even the partners of the Axis powers. Some of them even suggest that we should imitate the methods of the dictatorships. Americans never can and never will do that.

The experience of the past two years has proven beyond doubt that no nation can appease the Nazis. No man can tame a tiger into a kitten by stroking it. There can be no appeasement with ruthlessness. There can be no reasoning with an incendiary bomb. We know now that a nation can have peace with the Nazis only at the price of total surrender.

Even the people of Italy have been forced to become accomplices of the Nazis; but at this moment they do not know how soon they will be embraced to death by their allies.

The American appeasers ignore the warning to be found in the fate of Austria, Czechoslovakia, Poland, Norway, Belgium, the Netherlands, Denmark, and France.[3] They tell you that the Axis powers are going to win anyway; that all this bloodshed in the world could be saved; that the United States might just as well throw its influence into the scale of a dictated peace, and get the best out of it that we can.

They call it a "negotiated peace." Nonsense! Is it a negotiated peace if a gang of outlaws surrounds your community and on threat of extermination makes you pay tribute to save your own skins?

Such a dictated peace would be no peace at all. It would be only another armistice, leading to the most gigantic armament race and the most devastating

---

[2] The America First Committee, formed on September 4, 1940, urged that the United States not intervene in the war in Europe. At its high point, the America First Committee had 800,000 paid members. It disbanded on December 10, 1941.

[3] All of these countries had been taken over or conquered by Germany since 1938.

trade wars in all history. And in these contests the Americas would offer the only real resistance to the Axis powers.

With all their vaunted efficiency, with all their parade of pious purpose in this war, there are still in their background the concentration camp[4] and the servants of God in chains.

The history of recent years proves that shootings and chains and concentration camps are not simply the transient tools but the very altars of modern dictatorships. They may talk of a "new order" in the world, but what they have in mind is only a revival of the oldest and the worst tyranny. In that there is no liberty, no religion, no hope.

The proposed "new order" is the very opposite of a United States of Europe or a United States of Asia. It is not a Government based upon the consent of the governed. It is not a union of ordinary, self-respecting men and women to protect themselves and their freedom and their dignity from oppression. It is an unholy alliance of power and pelf to dominate and enslave the human race.

The British people and their allies today are conducting an active war against this unholy alliance. Our own future security is greatly dependent on the outcome of that fight. Our ability to "keep out of war" is going to be affected by that outcome.

Thinking in terms of today and tomorrow, I make the direct statement to the American people that there is far less chance of the United States getting into war, if we do all we can now to support the nations defending themselves against attack by the Axis than if we acquiesce in their defeat, submit tamely to an Axis victory, and wait our turn to be the object of attack in another war later on.

If we are to be completely honest with ourselves, we must admit that there is risk in any course we may take. But I deeply believe that the great majority of our people agree that the course that I advocate involves the least risk now and the greatest hope for world peace in the future.

The people of Europe who are defending themselves do not ask us to do their fighting. They ask us for the implements of war, the planes, the tanks, the guns, the freighters which will enable them to fight for their liberty and for our security. Emphatically we must get these weapons to them in sufficient volume

---

[4] The term "concentration camp" was first used to refer to any detention of people in a confined area by a political or military power. The Nazis began using concentration camps inside Germany to detain political opponents soon after coming to power.

and quickly enough, so that we and our children will be saved the agony and suffering of war which others have had to endure.

Let not the defeatists tell us that it is too late. It will never be earlier. Tomorrow will be later than today. Certain facts are self-evident.

In a military sense Great Britain and the British Empire are today the spearhead of resistance to world conquest. They are putting up a fight which will live forever in the story of human gallantry.

There is no demand for sending an American Expeditionary Force outside our own borders.[5] There is no intention by any member of your Government to send such a force. You can, therefore, nail any talk about sending armies to Europe as deliberate untruth.

Our national policy is not directed toward war. Its sole purpose is to keep war away from our country and our people. Democracy's fight against world conquest is being greatly aided, and must be more greatly aided, by the rearmament of the United States and by sending every ounce and every ton of munitions and supplies that we can possibly spare to help the defenders who are in the front lines. It is no more unneutral for us to do that than it is for Sweden, Russia and other nations near Germany, to send steel and ore and oil and other war materials into Germany every day in the week.

We are planning our own defense with the utmost urgency; and in its vast scale we must integrate the war needs of Britain and the other free nations which are resisting aggression.

This is not a matter of sentiment or of controversial personal opinion. It is a matter of realistic, practical military policy, based on the advice of our military experts who are in close touch with existing warfare. These military and naval experts and the members of the Congress and the Administration have a single-minded purpose – the defense of the United States.

This nation is making a great effort to produce everything that is necessary in this emergency – and with all possible speed. . . .

Nine days ago I announced the setting up of a more effective organization to direct our gigantic efforts to increase the production of munitions. The appropriation of vast sums of money and a well coordinated executive direction of our defense efforts are not in themselves enough. Guns, planes, ships and many other things have to be built in the factories and arsenals of America. They have to be produced by workers and managers and engineers

---

[5] American Expeditionary Force was the name of the wartime army that fought in Europe in World War I.

with the aid of machines which in turn have to be built by hundreds of thousands of workers throughout the land.

In this great work there has been splendid cooperation between the Government and industry and labor; and I am very thankful.

American industrial genius, unmatched throughout the world in the solution of production problems, has been called upon to bring its resources and its talents into action. Manufacturers of watches, farm implements, linotypes, cash registers, automobiles, sewing machines, lawn mowers and locomotives are now making fuses, bomb packing crates, telescope mounts, shells, pistols and tanks.

But all our present efforts are not enough. We must have more ships, more guns, more planes – more of everything. . . .

I appeal to the owners of plants – to the managers – to the workers – to our own Government employees – to put every ounce of effort into producing these munitions swiftly and without stint. With this appeal I give you the pledge that all of us who are officers of your Government will devote ourselves to the same whole-hearted extent to the great task that lies ahead.

As planes and ships and guns and shells are produced, your Government, with its defense experts, can then determine how best to use them to defend this hemisphere. The decision as to how much shall be sent abroad and how much shall remain at home must be made on the basis of our overall military necessities.

We must be the great arsenal of democracy. For us this is an emergency as serious as war itself. We must apply ourselves to our task with the same resolution, the same sense of urgency, the same spirit of patriotism and sacrifice as we would show were we at war. . . .

I have the profound conviction that the American people are now determined to put forth a mightier effort than they have ever yet made to increase our production of all the implements of defense, to meet the threat to our democratic faith.

As President of the United States I call for that national effort. I call for it in the name of this nation which we love and honor and which we are privileged and proud to serve. I call upon our people with absolute confidence that our common cause will greatly succeed.

Document 5

"The Four Freedoms"
Franklin D. Roosevelt
January 6, 1941

In his annual State of the Union Address to Congress on January 6, 1941, President Franklin D. Roosevelt reiterated the importance of supporting Great Britain in its war with Nazi Germany. In making his case, Roosevelt underscored the two nations' shared commitment to four universal freedoms. The "Four Freedoms" were subsequently formally incorporated into the Atlantic Charter crafted by Winston Churchill and FDR in August 1941 (Document 10). Once the United States entered the war on December 8, 1941, protecting these freedoms became the cornerstone of the American war effort.

Source: President Franklin Roosevelt's Annual Message (Four Freedoms) to Congress (1941), in 100 Milestone Documents, an online library compiled by the "Our Documents" Initiative, a cooperative effort of the National Archives and Records Administration with National History Day and USA Freedom Corps. https://goo.gl/9PmD2o

Mr. President, Mr. Speaker, Members of the Seventy-seventh Congress:

I address you, the Members of the Seventy-seventh Congress, at a moment unprecedented in the history of the Union. I use the word "unprecedented," because at no previous time has American security been as seriously threatened from without as it is today....

Even when the World War broke out in 1914, it seemed to contain only small threat of danger to our own American future. But, as time went on, the American people began to visualize what the downfall of democratic nations might mean to our own democracy.

We need not overemphasize imperfections in the Peace of Versailles. We need not harp on failure of the democracies to deal with problems of world reconstruction. We should remember that the Peace of 1919[1] was far less unjust than the kind of "pacification" which began even before Munich,[2] and which is being carried on under the new order of tyranny that seeks to spread over every continent today. The American people have unalterably set their faces against that tyranny.

Every realist knows that the democratic way of life is at this moment being directly assailed in every part of the world – assailed either by arms, or by secret spreading of poisonous propaganda by those who seek to destroy unity and promote discord in nations that are still at peace.

During sixteen long months this assault has blotted out the whole pattern of democratic life in an appalling number of independent nations, great and small. The assailants are still on the march, threatening other nations, great and small.

Therefore, as your President, performing my constitutional duty to "give to the Congress information of the state of the Union," I find it, unhappily, necessary to report that the future and the safety of our country and of our democracy are overwhelmingly involved in events far beyond our borders.

Armed defense of democratic existence is now being gallantly waged in four continents. If that defense fails, all the population and all the resources of Europe, Asia, Africa and Australasia will be dominated by the conquerors. Let us remember that the total of those populations and their resources in those four continents greatly exceeds the sum total of the population and the resources of the whole of the Western Hemisphere – many times over.

In times like these it is immature – and incidentally, untrue – for anybody to brag that an unprepared America, single-handed, and with one hand tied behind its back, can hold off the whole world.

No realistic American can expect from a dictator's peace international generosity, or return of true independence, or world disarmament, or freedom of expression, or freedom of religion – or even good business....

---

[1] By "Peace of 1919" and "Peace of Versailles" Roosevelt means the Treaty of Versailles, signed on June 28, 1919, which ended the war between Germany and the Allied Powers: principally Britain, France, and the United States. The terms of the treaty, particularly large reparation payments from Germany to the allies, were widely held to have caused many of the problems of the inter-war years and contributed to the rise of Nazism in Germany.

[2] The Munich Agreement, September 28, 1938, between Germany, Italy, France, and Great Britain allowed Germany to annex parts of Czechoslovakia. Germany occupied other parts of Czechoslovakia in March 1939, gaining significant industrial capacity and armaments. In September 1939, Germany invaded Poland.

The need of the moment is that our actions and our policy should be devoted primarily – almost exclusively – to meeting this foreign peril. For all our domestic problems are now a part of the great emergency.

Just as our national policy in internal affairs has been based upon a decent respect for the rights and the dignity of all our fellow men within our gates, so our national policy in foreign affairs has been based on a decent respect for the rights and dignity of all nations, large and small. And the justice of morality must and will win in the end. Our national policy is this:

First, by an impressive expression of the public will and without regard to partisanship, we are committed to all-inclusive national defense.

Second, by an impressive expression of the public will and without regard to partisanship, we are committed to full support of all those resolute peoples, everywhere, who are resisting aggression and are thereby keeping war away from our Hemisphere. By this support, we express our determination that the democratic cause shall prevail; and we strengthen the defense and the security of our own nation.

Third, by an impressive expression of the public will and without regard to partisanship, we are committed to the proposition that principles of morality and considerations for our own security will never permit us to acquiesce in a peace dictated by aggressors and sponsored by appeasers.

We know that enduring peace cannot be bought at the cost of other people's freedom.

In the recent national election there was no substantial difference between the two great parties in respect to that national policy. No issue was fought out on this line before the American electorate. Today it is abundantly evident that American citizens everywhere are demanding and supporting speedy and complete action in recognition of obvious danger.

Therefore, the immediate need is a swift and driving increase in our armament production....

A free nation has the right to expect full cooperation from all groups. A free nation has the right to look to the leaders of business, of labor, and of agriculture to take the lead in stimulating effort, not among other groups but within their own groups.

The best way of dealing with the few slackers or trouble makers in our midst is, first, to shame them by patriotic example, and, if that fails, to use the sovereignty of Government to save Government.

As men do not live by bread alone, they do not fight by armaments alone. Those who man our defenses, and those behind them who build our defenses, must have the stamina and the courage which come from unshakable belief in the manner of life which they are defending. The mighty action that we are calling for cannot be based on a disregard of all things worth fighting for.

The Nation takes great satisfaction and much strength from the things which have been done to make its people conscious of their individual stake in the preservation of democratic life in America. Those things have toughened the fiber of our people, have renewed their faith and strengthened their devotion to the institutions we make ready to protect.

Certainly this is no time for any of us to stop thinking about the social and economic problems which are the root cause of the social revolution which is today a supreme factor in the world.

For there is nothing mysterious about the foundations of a healthy and strong democracy. The basic things expected by our people of their political and economic systems are simple. They are:

Equality of opportunity for youth and for others.

Jobs for those who can work.

Security for those who need it.

The ending of special privilege for the few.

The preservation of civil liberties for all.

The enjoyment of the fruits of scientific progress in a wider and constantly rising standard of living.

These are the simple, basic things that must never be lost sight of in the turmoil and unbelievable complexity of our modern world. The inner and abiding strength of our economic and political systems is dependent upon the degree to which they fulfill these expectations.

Many subjects connected with our social economy call for immediate improvement. As examples:

We should bring more citizens under the coverage of old-age pensions and unemployment insurance.

We should widen the opportunities for adequate medical care.

We should plan a better system by which persons deserving or needing gainful employment may obtain it.

I have called for personal sacrifice. I am assured of the willingness of almost all Americans to respond to that call.

A part of the sacrifice means the payment of more money in taxes. In my Budget Message I shall recommend that a greater portion of this great defense program be paid for from taxation than we are paying today. No person should try, or be allowed, to get rich out of this program; and the principle of tax payments in accordance with ability to pay should be constantly before our eyes to guide our legislation.

If the Congress maintains these principles, the voters, putting patriotism ahead of pocketbooks, will give you their applause.

In the future days, which we seek to make secure, we look forward to a world founded upon four essential human freedoms.

The first is freedom of speech and expression – everywhere in the world.

The second is freedom of every person to worship God in his own way – everywhere in the world.

The third is freedom from want – which, translated into world terms, means economic understandings which will secure to every nation a healthy peacetime life for its inhabitants – everywhere in the world.

The fourth is freedom from fear – which, translated into world terms, means a world-wide reduction of armaments to such a point and in such a thorough fashion that no nation will be in a position to commit an act of physical aggression against any neighbor – anywhere in the world.

That is no vision of a distant millennium. It is a definite basis for a kind of world attainable in our own time and generation. That kind of world is the very antithesis of the so-called new order of tyranny which the dictators seek to create with the crash of a bomb.

To that new order we oppose the greater conception – the moral order. A good society is able to face schemes of world domination and foreign revolutions alike without fear.

Since the beginning of our American history, we have been engaged in change – in a perpetual peaceful revolution – a revolution which goes on steadily, quietly adjusting itself to changing conditions – without the concentration camp[3] or the quick-lime in the ditch. The world order which we seek is the cooperation of free countries, working together in a friendly, civilized society.

This nation has placed its destiny in the hands and heads and hearts of its millions of free men and women; and its faith in freedom under the guidance of God. Freedom means the supremacy of human rights everywhere. Our support goes to those who struggle to gain those rights or keep them. Our strength is our unity of purpose. To that high concept there can be no end save victory.

---

[3] The term "concentration camp" was first used to refer to any detention of people in a confined area by a political or military power. The Nazis began using concentration camps inside Germany to detain political opponents soon after coming to power.

Document 6

Gallup Polls
January 1940 – January 1941

In 1935 George Gallup's American Institute of Public Opinion began publishing public opinion polls based on modern scientific statistical sampling methods. Gallup viewed his polls as a way for the common man to speak directly to the government. His polls received wide distribution in American newspapers, raising questions about how much they influenced subsequent opinions among the public or politicians. Below are some examples of poll data Gallup collected to assess Americans' views about the European War between January 1940 and January 1941. During this period, President Franklin D. Roosevelt argued that Americans needed to offer economic aid to Britain to prevent Nazi Germany from attacking the United States.

We have edited Gallup's presentation of the data he collected. In some of his early polls, Gallup calculated the percentages of respondents who declined to answer a particular question as part of the total (100%) of all responses. In other cases, he noted the percentage of "no opinion" responses, yet excluded them from the overall calculation. In the latter cases, we use footnotes to avoid confusion.

Source: George H. Gallup, The Gallup Poll: Public Opinion 1935-1971, Vol. I: 1935-1948 (NY: Random House, 1972), p. 208, 211, 212, 225, 243, 250, 257, 259, and 262.

Do you think our country's future safety depends on England winning the war?
January 3, 1940

■ Yes ■ No ▫ No opinion

| 68% | 26% | 6% |

If the United States stopped sending war materials to England, do you think England would lose the war?
January 3, 1940

■ Yes ▫ No ▫ No opinion

| 85% | 8% | 7% |

If Germany tries to invade England within the next year, do you think she will be successful in conquering England?
January 3, 1940

■ Yes ▫ No ▫ No opinion

| 11% | 74% | 15% |

Do you think the United States will go into the war in Europe, or do you think we will stay out of the war?
February 16, 1940

■ Go into war ▫ Stay out

| 32% | 68% |

Why do you think the United States will stay out of the European war?
February 16, 1940

The three chief reasons given by those responding that the United States will stay out:

1. The people are overwhelmingly against war and would not stand for American participation.

2. The United States learned its lesson in the last war.

3. The nation would have everything to lose and nothing to gain.

If it appears that Germany is defeating England and France, should the United States declare war on Germany and send our army and navy to Europe to fight?[1]
February 21, 1940

■ Yes □ No

| 23% | 77% |

---

[1] Gallup reports that 7% of respondents had no opinion on this question. He excluded the "no opinion" responses before calculating the percentages for "Yes" and "No."

If it looked as though England and France would lose the war unless we loaned them money to buy war supplies here, would you favor or oppose lending them money?
March 4, 1940

■ Favor   □ Oppose

| 55% | 45% |

If Hitler offers to make peace this spring, do you think England and France should meet with the Germans and try to end the war?
March 10, 1940

■ Yes   □ No

| 75% | 25% |

Do you think now is the right time for the leading nations of the world to have a conference to try to settle Europe's problems and end the war between Germany and England and France?
March 10, 1940

■ Yes   □ No

| 58% | 42% |

If such a conference is held, should the United States take part in it?
March 10, 1940

■ Yes □ No

| 55% | 45% |

Which side do you want to see win the present war – England and France, or Germany?
March 31, 1940

■ England & France ■ Germany □ No opinion

| 84% | 1% | 15% |

Gallup Polls show the US want Britain to win. But we don't want to Actually fight.

If you were voting for President, which type of candidate would you be more likely to vote for: (A) A candidate who promises to keep us out of war and refuses to give any more help to England and France, even if they are being defeated by Germany (B) A can

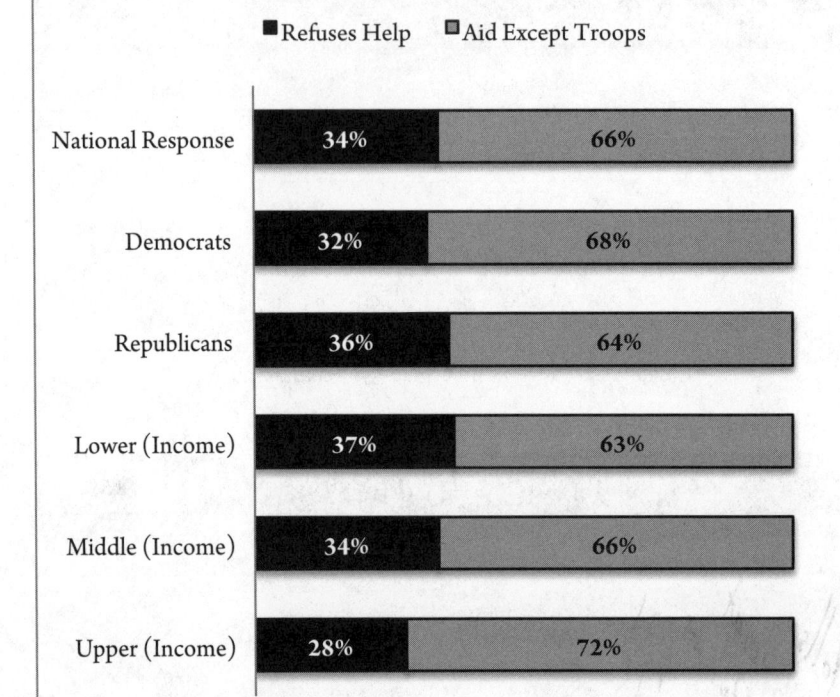

■ Refuses Help   ■ Aid Except Troops

Category	Refuses Help	Aid Except Troops
National Response	34%	66%
Democrats	32%	68%
Republicans	36%	64%
Lower (Income)	37%	63%
Middle (Income)	34%	66%
Upper (Income)	28%	72%

---

[2] Nine percent of respondents had no opinion on this question and are excluded from the overall calculation.

**Do you think the United States should increase
the size of its armed forces?**
May 22, 1940

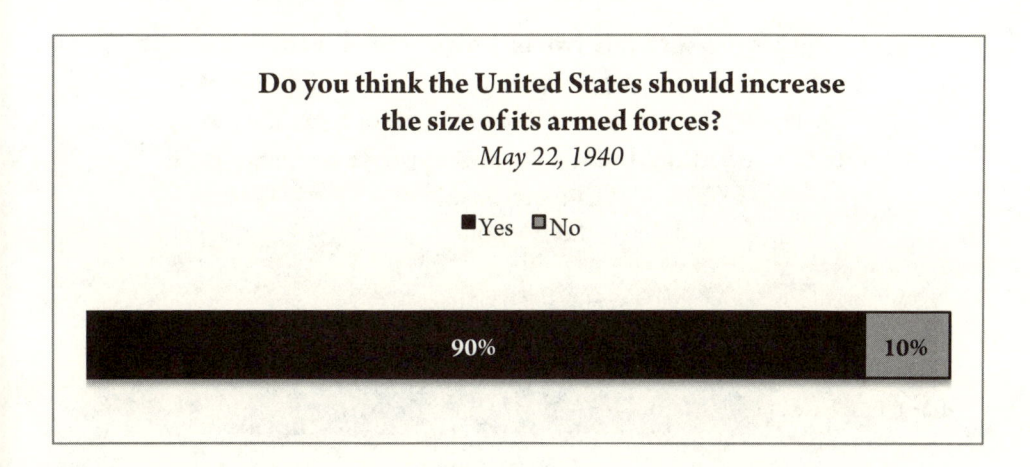

■Yes ◻No

| 90% | 10% |

**If England and France are unable to pay cash for airplanes
they buy in this country, do you think
we should sell them planes on credit supplied
by our government?[3]**
May 24, 1940

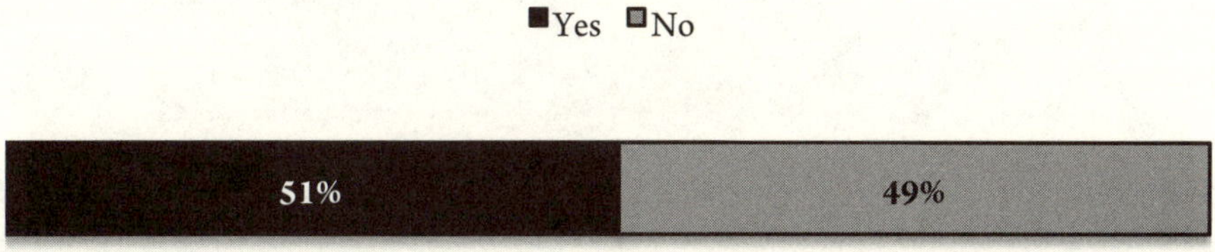

■Yes ◻No

| 51% | 49% |

---

[3] Six percent of respondents had no opinion on this question and are excluded from the overall calculation.

Congress has set aside two billion dollars for the army, navy, and air forces for the next 12 months. President Roosevelt has now asked Congress to increase this by another one billion dollars. Do you approve or disapprove of this increase?[4]

May 26, 1940

■ Approve ■ Disapprove

	Approve	Disapprove
National Response	86%	14%
Democrats	93%	7%
Republicans	83%	17%

---

[4] Five percent of respondents had no opinion on this question and are excluded from the overall calculation.

Would you be willing to pay a special tax to cover this increased expenditure?
May 26, 1940

■Yes ■No

Category	Yes	No
National Response	76%	24%
Lower (Income)	74%	26%
Middle (Income)	76%	24%
Upper (Income)	80%	20%

Do you think the United States should declare war on Germany and send our army and navy abroad to fight?
May 29, 1940

■Yes ■No

Yes	No
7%	93%

Do you think our country's army, navy, and air forces are strong enough so that the United States is safe from attack by any foreign nation?[5]

June 2, 1940

■ Yes □ No

| 15% | 85% |

---

[5] Ten percent of respondents had no opinion on this question and are excluded from the overall calculation.

Should the United States require every able bodied man who is 20 years old to serve in the army, navy, or the air force for one year?[6]

June 2, 1940

■ Yes   ▫ No

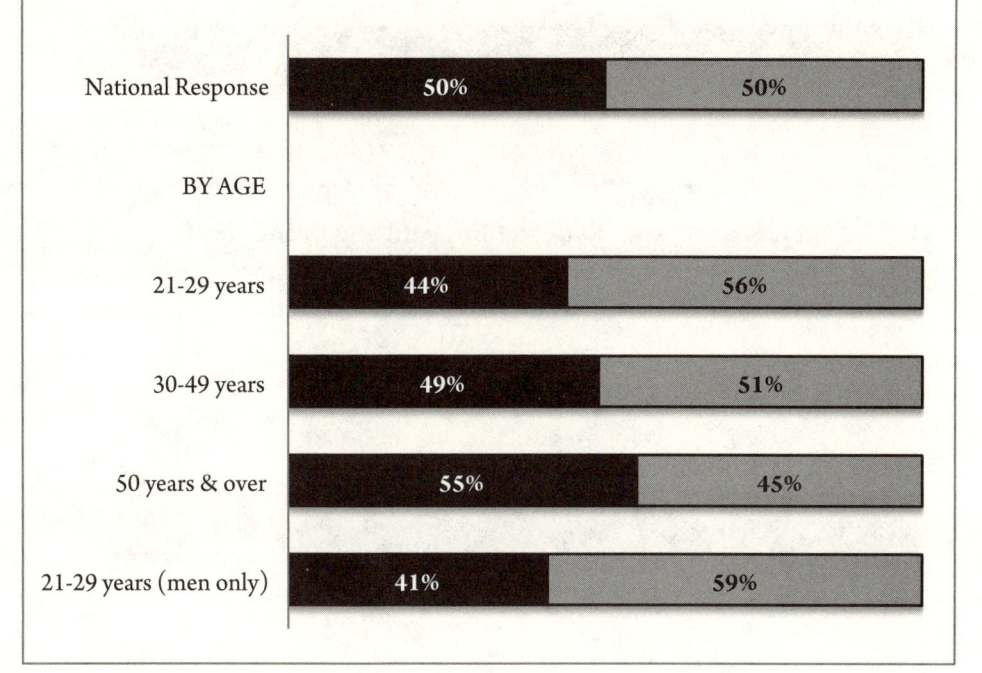

Category	Yes	No
National Response	50%	50%
BY AGE		
21-29 years	44%	56%
30-49 years	49%	51%
50 years & over	55%	45%
21-29 years (men only)	41%	59%

---

[6] The 7% of respondents who had no opinion on this question are excluded from the overall calculation.

Do you think that the C.C.C. camps should give military training to every young man in the C.C.C?[7]
June 2, 1940

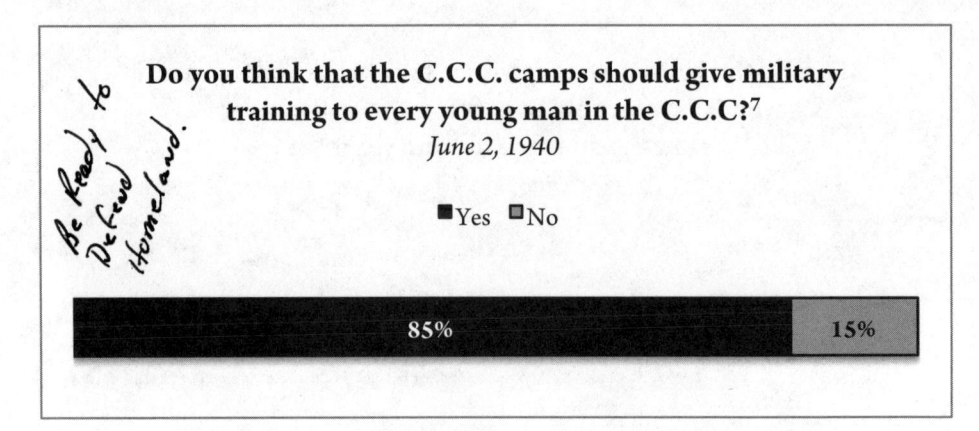

■Yes ☐No

(handwritten: Be Ready to Defend Homeland.)

| 85% | 15% |

If Germany should defeat England and France in the present war, do you think Germany would start a war against the United States sooner or later?[8]
June 2, 1940

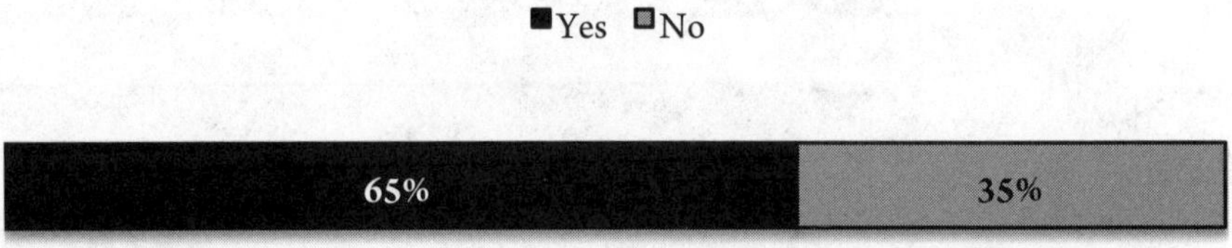

■Yes ☐No

| 65% | 35% |

---

[7] Again, 7% of respondents had no opinion on this question and are excluded from the overall calculation.

[8] The 10% of respondents who had no opinion on this question are excluded from the overall calculation.

Which of these two things do you think is the most important for the United States to try to do – to keep out of war ourselves or to help England win, even at the risk of getting into the war?[9]

September 23, 1940

■ Keep Out □ Help England

Region	Keep Out	Help England
National Response	48%	52%
BY REGION		
New England	48%	52%
Middle Atlantic	48%	52%
East Central	52%	48%
West Central	57%	43%
South	30%	70%
West	46%	54%

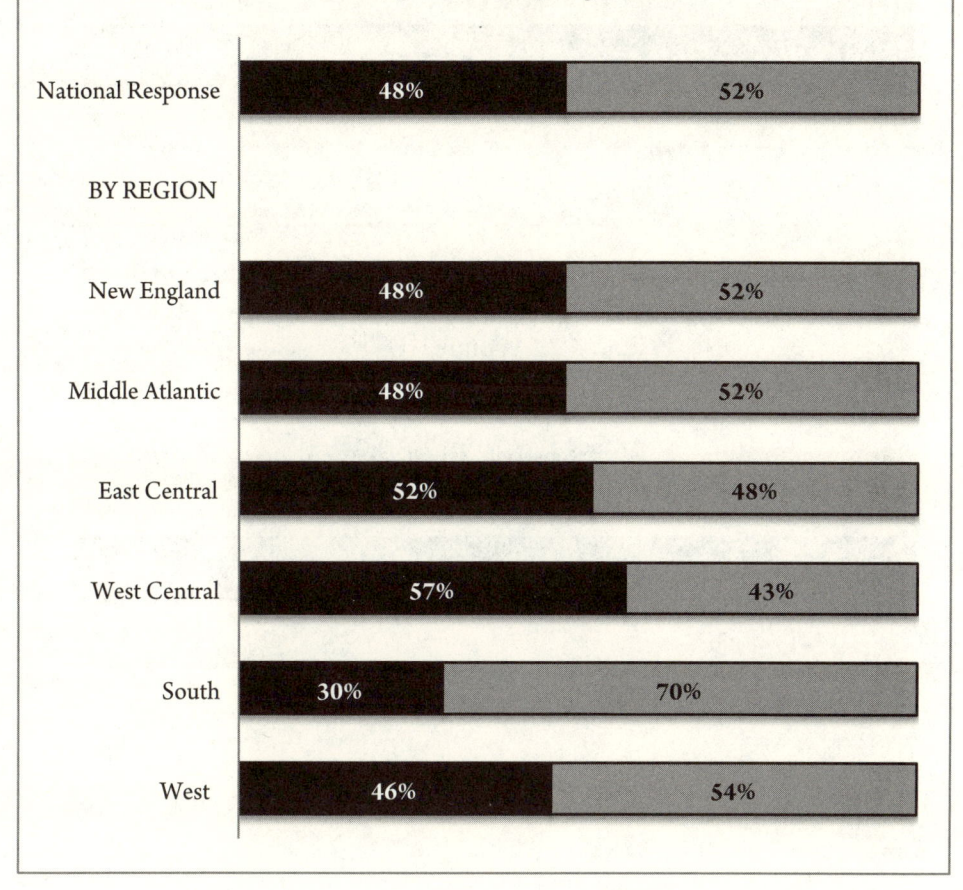

[9] Five percent of respondents had no opinion on this question and are excluded from the overall calculation.

Who do you think will do a better job of strenghtening our national defense – Roosevelt or Willkie?[10]

November 10, 1940

■ Roosevelt ▪ Willkie

Roosevelt	Willkie
61%	39%

If the United States should get into the war, which man would you prefer to have as President – Roosevelt or Willkie?[11]

November 10, 1940

■ Roosevelt ▪ Willkie

Roosevelt	Willkie
60%	40%

---

[10] The 13% of respondents who had no opinion on this question are excluded from the overall calculation.

[11] Nine percent of respondents had no opinion on this question. They are excluded from the overall calculation.

Gallup Polls 41

Asked in Great Britain: In view of the indiscriminate bombing of this country, would you approve or disapprove if the R.A.F adopted a similar policy of bombing the civilian population of Germany?
November 15, 1940

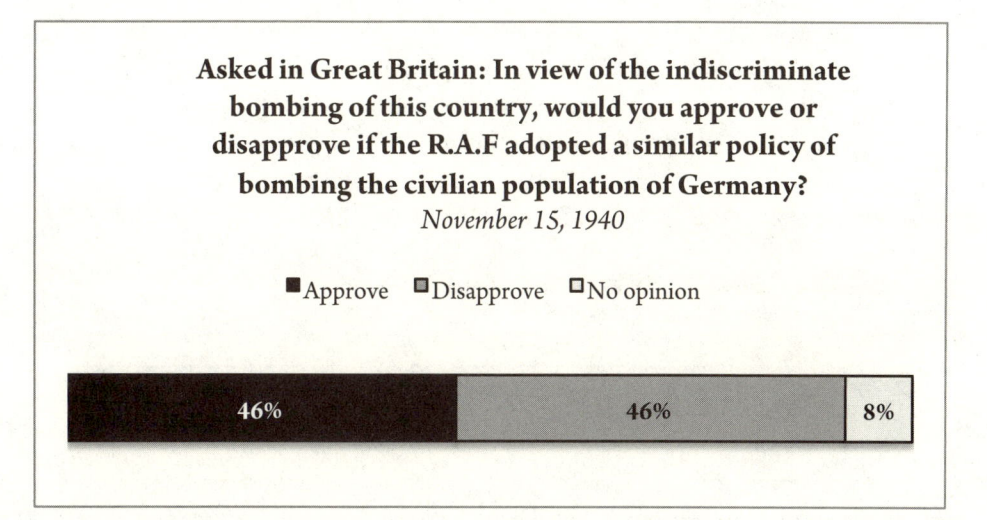

■ Approve ▨ Disapprove ▫ No opinion

| 46% | 46% | 8% |

If it appears that England will be defeated by Germany and Italy unless the United States supplies her with more food and war materials, would you be in favor of giving more help to England?[12]
November 18, 1940

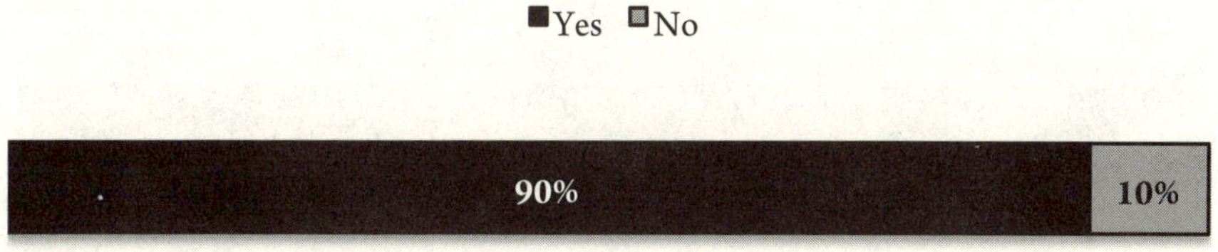

■ Yes ▫ No

| 90% | 10% |

---

[12] The 6% of respondents who had no opinion on this question are excluded from the overall calculation.

Which of these two things do you think is more important for the United States to try to do – to keep out of the war ourselves, or to help England win, even at the risk of getting into the war?
January 10, 1941

■ Keep Out □ Help England

| 40% | 60% |

If you were asked to vote on the question of the United States entering the war against Germany and Italy, how would you vote – to go into the war, or to stay out of the war?
January 10, 1941

■ Go In □ Stay Out

| 12% | 88% |

Do you think it was a mistake for the United States to enter the last World War?
January 10, 1941

■ Yes □ No □ No opinion

| 39% | 42% | 19% |

If the British are unable to pay cash for war materials bought in this country, should our Government lend or lease war materials to the British, to be paid back in the same materials and other goods after the war is over?
January 22, 1941

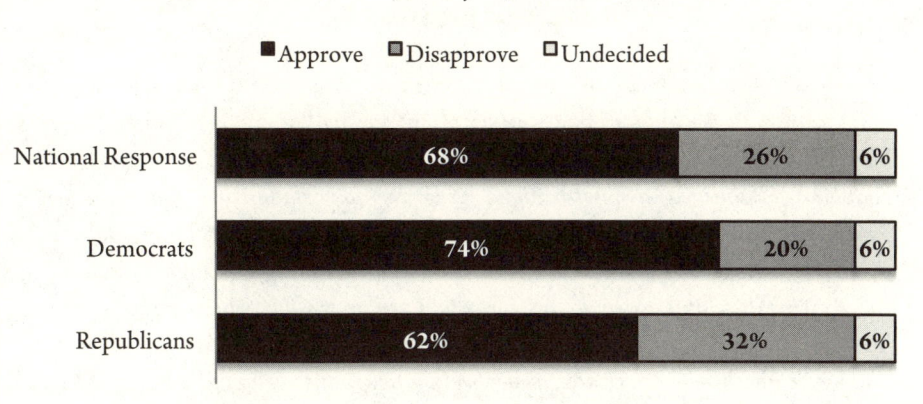

■ Approve   ▨ Disapprove   □ Undecided

	Approve	Disapprove	Undecided
National Response	68%	26%	6%
Democrats	74%	20%	6%
Republicans	62%	32%	6%

Which of these two things do you think England should do now – try to make the best possible peace now with Germany, or keep on fighting in the hope of defeating Germany?
January 31, 1941

■ Make peace now   ▨ Keep on fighting   □ No opinion

Make peace now	Keep on fighting	No opinion
15%	79%	6%

Document 7

The First Lady Visits Tuskegee
Eleanor Roosevelt
April 1, 1941

If war came, African Americans wanted to ensure that they had equal opportunities in the military and workplace. In World War I, there were no black pilots in the American Air Service. In 1941, the Tuskegee Institute in Tuskegee, Alabama established a pilot-training program to demonstrate that African Americans had the mental and physical stamina to fly. First Lady Eleanor Roosevelt, a stalwart supporter of equal rights, helped Tuskegee secure a loan from the Rosenwald Fund to build an airfield. Even more importantly, she visited Tuskegee and took a well-publicized flight with instructor Charles Alfred Anderson. She wrote about her experiences in her weekly newspaper column, "My Day." (A photo of her sitting in the plane behind Anderson appears on page 79.) Once war was declared, the Tuskegee airmen became the first black pilots in the American armed forces and served with distinction.

Source: *Eleanor Roosevelt, My Day: A Comprehensive, Electronic Edition of Eleanor Roosevelt's "My Day" Columns. Online by the Eleanor Roosevelt Papers, Project of the Department of History at George Washington University.* https://goo.gl/NvuBQM

GREENSBORO, N.C., Monday—One of the interesting things we saw near Tuskegee was a real rural theatre. The actors had built the stage and arranged the room for the audience. There were rough benches, an open fire, and some very interesting masks for decoration on the walls. It was called "The Bucket Theatre," and on the sign outside was a quotation from Booker T.

Washington which read: "Put your bucket down where you are."[1] This little rural theatre certainly is putting down its bucket in that community.

Saturday morning the Tuskegee Institute trustees met again all morning, and in the afternoon we visited the hospital, listened to the health problems which Tuskegee is trying to ameliorate. I had the pleasure of going through the new unit for the treatment of infantile paralysis which has been installed here by the National Foundation for Infantile Paralysis. I am taking back a book full of pictures so that the President, who is much interested in the installment of this unit, will have an opportunity to see what it looks like. . . .

Finally we went out to the aviation field, where a Civil Aeronautics unit for the teaching of colored pilots is in full swing. They have advanced training here, and some of the students went up and did acrobatic flying for us. These boys[2] are good pilots. I had the fun of going up in one of the tiny training planes with the head instructor, and seeing this interesting countryside from the air.

The days at Tuskegee have given me much to think about. To see a group of people working together for improvement of undesirable conditions is very heartening. . . .

---

[1] Booker T. Washington founded Tuskegee Institute in 1881. This quote, from his 1895 "Atlanta Compromise" address, summarized his advice to African Americans in the difficult Southern post-Reconstruction era that they seek the respect of their white neighbors by learning the skills demanded by commerce. During Washington's leadership, the Institute emphasized the teaching of manual trades such as bricklaying and carpentry, along with agriculture and domestic arts.

[2] In referring to the pilots as "boys," Mrs. Roosevelt is using a term universally applied to American soldiers, sailors, and airmen during World War II.

Document 8

"America First"
Charles Lindbergh
April 23, 1941

Charles Lindbergh became one of the most famous men in America when he completed the first-ever solo flight from New York to Paris in 1927. By the late thirties, Lindbergh had evolved into a more controversial figure, after he expressed admiration for Nazi Germany. He also served as a prominent spokesman for the America First Committee, a group that formed in September 1940 to oppose intervention in the European War. Lindbergh delivered this address at an America First Committee meeting in New York City on April 23, 1941.

Source: The text of Colonel Lindbergh's Address at a Rally of the America First Committee, New York Times (1923-Current file); Apr 24, 1941; ProQuest Historical Newspapers: The New York Times, p. 12. https://goo.gl/EAbntf

---

... I have said before, and I will say again, that I believe it will be a tragedy to the entire world if the British Empire collapses. That is one of the main reasons why I opposed this war before it was declared, and why I have constantly advocated a negotiated peace. I did not feel that England and France had a reasonable chance of winning. France has now been defeated; and, despite the propaganda and confusion of recent months, it is now obvious that England is losing the war. I believe this is realized even by the British government. But they have one last desperate plan remaining. They hope that they may be able to persuade us to send another American Expeditionary Force[1] to Europe, and to share with England militarily, as well as financially, the fiasco of this war.

I do not blame England for this hope, or for asking for our assistance. But we now know that she declared a war under circumstances [that] led to the defeat of every nation that sided with her from Poland to Greece. We know

---

[1] The name given to the American military force that fought in Europe in World War I.

that in the desperation of war England promised to all these nations armed assistance that she could not send. We know that she misinformed them, as she has misinformed us, concerning her state of preparation, her military strength, and the progress of the war.

In time of war, truth is always replaced by propaganda. I do not believe we should be too quick to criticize the actions of a belligerent nation. There is always the question whether we, ourselves, would do better under similar circumstances. But we in this country have a right to think of the welfare of America first, just as the people in England thought first of their own country when they encouraged the smaller nations of Europe to fight against hopeless odds. When England asks us to enter this war, she is considering her own future, and that of her Empire. In making our reply, I believe we should consider the future of the United States and that of the Western Hemisphere.

It is not only our right, but it is our obligation as American citizens to look at this war objectively, and to weigh our chances for success if we should enter it. I have attempted to do this, especially from the standpoint of aviation; and I have been forced to the conclusion that we cannot win this war for England, regardless of how much assistance we extend.

I ask you to look at the map of Europe today and see if you can suggest any way in which we could win this war if we entered it. Suppose we had a large army in America, trained and equipped. Where would we send it to fight? The campaigns of the war show only too clearly how difficult it is to force a landing, or to maintain an army, on a hostile coast. Suppose we took our navy from the Pacific, and used it to convoy British shipping. That would not win the war for England. It would, at best, permit her to exist under the constant bombing of the German air fleet. Suppose we had an air force that we could send to Europe. Where could it operate? Some of our squadrons might be based in the British Isles; but it is physically impossible to base enough aircraft in the British Isles alone to equal in strength the aircraft that can be based on the continent of Europe.

I have asked these questions on the supposition that we had in existence an army and an air force large enough and well enough equipped to send to Europe; and that we would dare to remove our navy from the Pacific. Even on this basis, I do not see how we could invade the continent of Europe successfully as long as all of that continent and most of Asia is under Axis[2] domination. But the fact is that none of these suppositions are correct. We

---

[2] "Axis" was the name given to the alliance of Germany, Japan, and Italy, which also included some other countries, such as Bulgaria and Hungary.

have only a one-ocean navy. Our army is still untrained and inadequately equipped for foreign war. Our air force is deplorably lacking in modern fighting planes.

When these facts are cited, the interventionists shout that we are defeatists, that we are undermining the principles of Democracy, and that we are giving comfort to Germany by talking about our military weakness. But everything I mention here has been published in our newspapers, and in the reports of congressional hearings in Washington. Our military position is well known to the governments of Europe and Asia. Why, then, should it not be brought to the attention of our own people?...

When history is written, the responsibility for the downfall of the democracies of Europe will rest squarely upon the shoulders of the interventionists who led their nations into war uninformed and unprepared....

There are many such interventionists in America, but there are more people among us of a different type. That is why you and I are assembled here tonight. There is a policy open to this nation that will lead to success – a policy that leaves us free to follow our own way of life, and to develop our own civilization. It is not a new and untried idea. It was advocated by Washington. It was incorporated in the Monroe Doctrine.[3] Under its guidance, the United States became the greatest nation in the world. It is based upon the belief that the security of a nation lies in the strength and character of its own people. It recommends the maintenance of armed forces sufficient to defend this hemisphere from attack by any combination of foreign powers. It demands faith in an independent American destiny. This is the policy of the America First Committee today. It is a policy not of isolation, but of independence; not of defeat, but of courage. It is a policy that led this nation to success during the most trying years of our history, and it is a policy that will lead us to success again.

We have weakened ourselves for many months, and still worse, we have divided our own people by this dabbling in Europe's wars. While we should have been concentrating on American defense, we have been forced to argue over foreign quarrels. We must turn our eyes and our faith back to our own country before it is too late. And when we do this, a different vista opens before us. Practically every difficulty we would face in invading Europe becomes an asset to us in defending America. Our enemy, and not we, would then have the

---

[3] Announced in 1823 by President James Monroe, this policy stated that the United States would not involve itself in the affairs of Europe, while warning European nations against interfering in the affairs of the western hemisphere.

problem of transporting millions of troops across the ocean and landing them on a hostile shore. They, and not we, would have to furnish the convoys to transport guns and trucks and munitions and fuel across three thousand miles of water. Our battleships and submarines would then be fighting close to their home bases. We would then do the bombing from the air, and the torpedoing at sea. And if any part of an enemy convoy should ever pass our navy and our air force, they would still be faced with the guns of our coast artillery, and behind them, the divisions of our army.

The United States is better situated from a military standpoint than any other nation in the world. Even in our present condition of unpreparedness, no foreign power is in a position to invade us today. If we concentrate on our own and build the strength that this nation should maintain, no foreign army will ever attempt to land on American shores....

During the last several years, I have travelled over this country, from one end to the other. I have talked to many hundreds of men and women, and I have had letters from tens of thousands more, who feel the same way as you and I. Most of these people have no influence or power. Most of them have no means of expressing their convictions, except by their vote which has always been against this war. They are the citizens who have had to work too hard at their daily jobs to organize political meetings. Hitherto, they have relied upon their vote to express their feelings; but now they find that it is hardly remembered except in the oratory of a political campaign. These people – the majority of hard-working American citizens – are with us. They are the true strength of our country. And they are beginning to realize, as you and I, that there are times when we must sacrifice our normal interests in life in order to insure the safety and the welfare of our nation.

Such a time has come. Such a crisis is here. That is why the America First Committee has been formed – to give voice to the people who have no newspaper, or news reel, or radio station at their command; to the people who must do the paying, and the fighting, and the dying, if this country enters the war....

Whether or not we do enter the war, rests upon the shoulders of you in this audience, upon us here on this platform, upon meetings of this kind that are being held by Americans in every section of the United States today. It depends upon the action we take, and the courage we show at this time. If you believe in an independent destiny for America, if you believe that this country should not enter the war in Europe, we ask you to join the America First Committee in its stand. We ask you to share our faith in the ability of this nation to defend itself, to develop its own civilization, and to contribute to the progress of mankind in a more constructive and intelligent way than has yet been found by the warring nations of Europe. We need your support, and we need it now. The time to act is here.

Document 9

Executive Order 8802 – Prohibition of Discrimination in the Defense Industry
Franklin D. Roosevelt
June 25, 1941

President Franklin D. Roosevelt's decision to make the United States the "arsenal of democracy," as he announced in his fireside chat on December 29, 1940 (Document 4), created numerous high-paying jobs in manufacturing. Yet racial discrimination prevented many African Americans from securing these jobs. In 1941, the labor leader A. Philip Randolph began planning a mass march on Washington, DC to pressure Roosevelt to act. To avoid the embarrassment of a march that showcased American racial problems to the world, Roosevelt convinced Randolph to call off the march in return for Executive Order 8802. Dubbed the "Second Emancipation Proclamation," EO 8802 was the first time since Reconstruction that the federal government had acted to explicitly protect the rights of African Americans.

Source: "Executive Order 8802," in 100 Milestone Documents, *an online library compiled by the "Our Documents" Initiative, a cooperative effort of the National Archives and Records Administration with National History Day and USA Freedom Corps. https://goo.gl/VUHPqx*

Whereas it is the policy of the United States to encourage full participation in the national defense program by all citizens of the United States, regardless of race, creed, color, or national origin, in the firm belief that the democratic way of life within the Nation can be defended successfully only with the help and support of all groups within its borders; and

Whereas there is evidence that available and needed workers have been barred from employment in industries engaged in defense production solely because of consideration of race, creed, color, or national origin, to the detriment of workers' morale and of national unity:

Now, Therefore, by virtue of the authority vested in me by the Constitution and the statutes, and as a prerequisite to the successful conduct of our national defense production effort, I do hereby reaffirm the policy of the United States that there shall be no discrimination in the employment of workers in defense industries or government because of race, creed, color, or national origin, and I do hereby declare that it is the duty of employers and of labor organizations, in furtherance of said policy and of this Order, to provide for the full and equitable participation of all workers in defense industries, without discrimination because of race, creed, color, or national origin;

And it is hereby ordered as follows:

1. All departments and agencies of the Government of the United States concerned with vocational and training programs for defense production shall take special measures appropriate to assure that such programs are administered without discrimination because of race, creed, color, or national origin;

2. All contracting agencies of the Government of the United States shall include in all defense contracts hereafter negotiated by them a provision obligating the contractor not to discriminate against any worker because of race, creed, color, or national origin;

3. There is established in the Office of Production Management[1] a Committee on Fair Employment Practice, which shall consist of a Chairman and four other members to be appointed by the President. The Chairman and members of the Committee shall serve as such without compensation but shall be entitled to actual and necessary transportation, subsistence, and other expenses incidental to performance of their duties. The Committee shall receive and investigate complaints of discrimination in violation of the provisions of this Order and shall take appropriate steps to redress grievances which it finds to be valid. The Committee shall also recommend to the several departments and agencies of the Government of the United States and to the President all measures which may be deemed by it necessary or proper to effectuate the provisions of this Order.

Franklin D. Roosevelt

---

[1] Created in 1941, the Office of Production Management was supposed to assist in the conversion from peacetime to wartime industrial production. It became part of the War Production Board when that agency was established in 1942.

Document 10

The Atlantic Charter
August 14, 1941

In August 1941 (four months before the United States entered the war), President Franklin D. Roosevelt and British Prime Minister Winston Churchill met in Newfoundland and crafted the Atlantic Charter. In June, Nazi Germany had invaded the Soviet Union, making Great Britain and the Soviet Union allies. The Atlantic Charter, however, envisioned the world's leading democracies, not communist Russia, re-building the postwar world. The Atlantic Charter remained the fundamental statement of American war aims. The Charter's call for self-government and self-determination also inadvertently became touchstones for those around the world wishing for independence from European empires.

Source: "The Atlantic Charter," National Archives and Records Administration, Records of the Office of Government Reports, Record Group 44. https://goo.gl/TR6E3F

The President of the United States of America and the Prime Minister, Mr. Churchill, representing His Majesty's Government in the United Kingdom, being met together, deem it right to make known certain common principles in the national policies of their respective countries on which they base their hopes for a better future for the world.

First, their countries seek no aggrandizement, territorial or other;

Second, they desire to see no territorial changes that do not accord with the freely expressed wishes of the peoples concerned;

Third, they respect the right of all peoples to choose the form of government under which they will live; and they wish to see sovereign rights and self-government restored to those who have been forcibly deprived of them;

Fourth, they will endeavor, with due respect for their existing obligations, to further the enjoyment by all States, great or small, victor or vanquished, of access, on equal terms, to the trade and to the raw materials of the world which are needed for their economic prosperity;

Fifth, they desire to bring about the fullest collaboration between all nations in the economic field with the object of securing, for all, improved labor standards, economic advancement and social security;

Sixth, after the final destruction of the Nazi tyranny, they hope to see established a peace which will afford to all nations the means of dwelling in safety within their own boundaries, and which will afford assurance that all the men in all lands may live out their lives in freedom from fear and want;

Seventh, such a peace should enable all men to traverse the high seas and oceans without hindrance;

Eighth, they believe that all of the nations of the world, for realistic as well as spiritual reasons must come to the abandonment of the use of force. Since no future peace can be maintained if land, sea or air armaments continue to be employed by nations which threaten, or may threaten, aggression outside of their frontiers, they believe, pending the establishment of a wider and permanent system of general security, that the disarmament of such nations is essential. They will likewise aid and encourage all other practicable measures which will lighten for peace-loving peoples the crushing burden of armaments.

Franklin D. Roosevelt
Winston S. Churchill

Document 11

Fireside Chat on the *Greer* Incident
Franklin D. Roosevelt
September 11, 1941

Lend-Lease (Document 3) solved Great Britain's credit problems in securing American food and ammunition, but American law still required Britain to transport these goods in its own ships. German submarines patrolling the Atlantic sank many British transports. On September 4, 1941, a German submarine sank the Greer, an American destroyer. In this Fireside chat, President Franklin D. Roosevelt rejected the German claim that it had mistaken the Greer for a British ship. He used the incident to order U.S. naval ships to escort British transports as far as Iceland and to fire on sight at any German ship or submarine. Non-interventionists objected, claiming that Roosevelt was fighting an undeclared naval war against Germany in the Atlantic Ocean.

Source: Franklin D. Roosevelt, "Fireside Chat" (September 11, 1941), Online by Gerhard Peters and John T. Woolley, The American Presidency Project. https://goo.gl/YS3DUC.

Navy Department of the United States has reported to me that on the morning of September fourth the United States destroyer *Greer*, proceeding in full daylight toward Iceland, had reached a point southeast of Greenland. She was carrying American mail to Iceland. She was flying the American flag. Her identity as an American ship was unmistakable.

She was then and there attacked by a submarine. Germany admits that it was a German submarine. The submarine deliberately fired a torpedo at the Greer, followed later by another torpedo attack. In spite of what Hitler's propaganda bureau has invented, and in spite of what any American obstructionist organization may prefer to believe, I tell you the blunt fact that the German submarine fired first upon this American destroyer without warning, and with deliberate design to sink her.

Our destroyer, at the time, was in waters which the Government of the United States had declared to be waters of self-defense – surrounding outposts of American protection in the Atlantic.

In the North of the Atlantic, outposts have been established by us in Iceland, in Greenland, in Labrador and in Newfoundland. Through these waters there pass many ships of many flags. They bear food and other supplies to civilians; and they bear materiel of war, for which the people of the United States are spending billions of dollars, and which, by Congressional action, they have declared to be essential for the defense of our own land.

The United States destroyer, when attacked, was proceeding on a legitimate mission.

If the destroyer was visible to the submarine when the torpedo was fired, then the attack was a deliberate attempt by the Nazis to sink a clearly identified American warship. On the other hand, if the submarine was beneath the surface of the sea and, with the aid of its listening devices, fired in the direction of the sound of the American destroyer without even taking the trouble to learn its identity – as the official German communique would indicate – then the attack was even more outrageous. For it indicates a policy of indiscriminate violence against any vessel sailing the seas – belligerent or non-belligerent.

This was piracy – piracy legally and morally. It was not the first nor the last act of piracy which the Nazi Government has committed against the American flag in this war. For attack has followed attack. . . .

Four . . . vessels sunk or attacked flew the American flag and were clearly identifiable. Two of these ships were warships of the American Navy. In the fifth case, the vessel sunk clearly carried the flag of our sister Republic of Panama.

In the face of all this, we Americans are keeping our feet on the ground. Our type of democratic civilization has outgrown the thought of feeling compelled to fight some other Nation by reason of any single piratical attack on one of our ships. We are not becoming hysterical or losing our sense of proportion. Therefore, what I am thinking and saying tonight does not relate to any isolated episode.

Instead, we Americans are taking a long-range point of view in regard to certain fundamentals and to a series of events on land and on sea which must be considered as a whole – as a part of a world pattern.

It would be unworthy of a great Nation to exaggerate an isolated incident, or to become inflamed by some one act of violence. But it would be inexcusable folly to minimize such incidents in the face of evidence which makes it clear that the incident is not isolated, but is part of a general plan.

The important truth is that these acts of international lawlessness are a manifestation of a design which has been made clear to the American people for a long time. It is the Nazi design to abolish the freedom of the seas, and to acquire absolute control and domination of these seas for themselves.

For with control of the seas in their own hands, the way can obviously become clear for their next step – domination of the United States – domination of the Western Hemisphere by force of arms. Under Nazi control of the seas, no merchant ship of the United States or of any other American Republic would be free to carry on any peaceful commerce, except by the condescending grace of this foreign and tyrannical power. The Atlantic Ocean which has been, and which should always be, a free and friendly highway for us would then become a deadly menace to the commerce of the United States, to the coasts of the United States, and even to the inland cities of the United States.

The Hitler Government, in defiance of the laws of the sea, in defiance of the recognized rights of all other Nations, has presumed to declare, on paper, that great areas of the seas – even including a vast expanse lying in the Western Hemisphere – are to be closed, and that no ships may enter them for any purpose, except at peril of being sunk. Actually they are sinking ships at will and without warning in widely separated areas both within and far outside of these far-flung pretended zones.

This Nazi attempt to seize control of the oceans is but a counterpart of the Nazi plots now being carried on throughout the Western Hemisphere – all designed toward the same end. For Hitler's advance guards – not only his avowed agents but also his dupes among us – have sought to make ready for him footholds and bridgeheads in the New World, to be used as soon as he has gained control of the oceans....

To be ultimately successful in world mastery, Hitler knows that he must get control of the seas. He must first destroy the bridge of ships which we are building across the Atlantic and over which we shall continue to roll the implements of war to help destroy him, to destroy all his works in the end. He must wipe out our patrol on sea and in the air if he is to do it. He must silence the British Navy.

I think it must be explained over and over again to people who like to think of the United States Navy as an invincible protection, that this can be true only if the British Navy survives. And that, my friends, is simple arithmetic.

For if the world outside of the Americas falls under Axis[1] domination, the shipbuilding facilities which the Axis powers would then possess in all of Europe, in the British Isles, and in the Far East would be much greater than all the shipbuilding facilities and potentialities of all of the Americas – not only greater, but two or three times greater – enough to win. Even if the United States threw all its resources into such a situation, seeking to double and even redouble the size of our Navy, the Axis powers, in control of the rest of the world, would have the manpower and the physical resources to out build us several times over.

It is time for all Americans, Americans of all the Americas to stop being deluded by the romantic notion that the Americas can go on living happily and peacefully in a Nazi-dominated world.

Generation after generation, America has battled for the general policy of the freedom of the seas. And that policy is a very simple one – but a basic, a fundamental one. It means that no Nation has the right to make the broad oceans of the world at great distances from the actual theater of land war unsafe for the commerce of others.

That has been our policy, proved time and time again, in all our history.

Our policy has applied from the earliest days of the Republic – and still applies – not merely to the Atlantic but to the Pacific and to all other oceans as well.

Unrestricted submarine warfare in 1941 constitutes a defiance – an act of aggression – against that historic American policy.

It is now clear that Hitler has begun his campaign to control the seas by ruthless force and by wiping out every vestige of international law, every vestige of humanity.

His intention has been made clear. The American people can have no further illusions about it.

No tender whisperings of appeasers that Hitler is not interested in the Western Hemisphere, no soporific lullabies that a wide ocean protects us from him – can long have any effect on the hard-headed, far-sighted, and realistic American people.

Because of these episodes, because of the movements and operations of German warships, and because of the clear, repeated proof that the present Government of Germany has no respect for treaties or for international law, that it has no decent attitude toward neutral Nations or human life – we

---

[1] The name given to the alliance of Germany, Japan, and Italy, which also included some other countries, such as Bulgaria and Hungary.

Americans are now face to face not with abstract theories but with cruel, relentless facts.

This attack on the Greer was no localized military operation in the North Atlantic. This was no mere episode in a struggle between two Nations. This was one determined step toward creating a permanent world system based on force, on terror, and on murder.

And I am sure that even now the Nazis are waiting to see whether the United States will by silence give them the green light to go ahead on this path of destruction.

The Nazi danger to our Western world has long ceased to be a mere possibility. The danger is here now – not only from a military enemy but from an enemy of all law, all liberty, all morality, all religion.

There has now come a time when you and I must see the cold, inexorable necessity of saying to these inhuman, unrestrained seekers of world conquest and permanent world domination by the sword: "You seek to throw our children and our children's children into your form of terrorism and slavery. You have now attacked our own safety. You shall go no further."

Normal practices of diplomacy – note writing – are of no possible use in dealing with international outlaws who sink our ships and kill our citizens.

One peaceful Nation after another has met disaster because each refused to look the Nazi danger squarely in the eye until it actually had them by the throat.

The United States will not make that fatal mistake.

No act of violence, no act of intimidation will keep us from maintaining intact two bulwarks of American defense: First, our line of supply of materiel to the enemies of Hitler; and second, the freedom of our shipping on the high seas.

No matter what it takes, no matter what it costs, we will keep open the line of legitimate commerce in these defensive waters.

We have sought no shooting war with Hitler. We do not seek it now. But neither do we want peace so much, that we are willing to pay for it by permitting him to attack our naval and merchant ships while they are on legitimate business.

I assume that the German leaders are not deeply concerned, tonight or any other time, by what we Americans or the American Government say or publish about them. We cannot bring about the downfall of Nazism by the use of long-range invective.

But when you see a rattlesnake poised to strike, you do not wait until he has struck before you crush him.

These Nazi submarines and raiders are the rattlesnakes of the Atlantic. They are a menace to the free pathways of the high seas. They are a challenge to our sovereignty. They hammer at our most precious rights when they attack ships of the American flag – symbols of our independence, our freedom, our very life.

It is clear to all Americans that the time has come when the Americas themselves must now be defended. A continuation of attacks in our own waters, or in waters that could be used for further and greater attacks on us, will inevitably weaken our American ability to repel Hitlerism.

Do not let us be hair-splitters. Let us not ask ourselves whether the Americas should begin to defend themselves after the first attack, or the fifth attack, or the tenth attack, or the twentieth attack.

The time for active defense is now.

Do not let us split hairs. Let us not say: "We will only defend ourselves if the torpedo succeeds in getting home, or if the crew and the passengers are drowned."

This is the time for prevention of attack.

If submarines or raiders attack in distant waters, they can attack equally well within sight of our own shores. Their very presence in any waters which America deems vital to its defense constitutes an attack.

In the waters which we deem necessary for our defense, American naval vessels and American planes will no longer wait until Axis submarines lurking under the water, or Axis raiders on the surface of the sea, strike their deadly blow – first.

Upon our naval and air patrol – now operating in large number over a vast expanse of the Atlantic Ocean – falls the duty of maintaining the American policy of freedom of the seas – now. That means, very simply, very clearly, that our patrolling vessels and planes will protect all merchant ships – not only American ships but ships of any flag – engaged in commerce in our defensive waters. They will protect them from submarines; they will protect them from surface raiders.

This situation is not new. The second President of the United States, John Adams, ordered the United States Navy to clean out European privateers and European ships of war which were infesting the Caribbean and South American waters, destroying American commerce.

The third President of the United States, Thomas Jefferson, ordered the United States Navy to end the attacks being made upon American and other ships by the corsairs of the Nations of North Africa.

My obligation as President is historic; it is clear. It is inescapable. It is no act of war on our part when we decide to protect the seas that are vital to American defense. The aggression is not ours. Ours is solely defense.

But let this warning be clear. From now on, if German or Italian vessels of war enter the waters, the protection of which is necessary for American defense, they do so at their own peril.

The orders which I have given as Commander in Chief of the United States Army and Navy are to carry out that policy – at once.

The sole responsibility rests upon Germany. There will be no shooting unless Germany continues to seek it.

That is my obvious duty in this crisis. That is the clear right of this sovereign Nation. This is the only step possible, if we would keep tight the wall of defense which we are pledged to maintain around this Western Hemisphere.

I have no illusions about the gravity of this step. I have not taken it hurriedly or lightly. It is the result of months and months of constant thought and anxiety and prayer. In the protection of your Nation and mine it cannot be avoided.

The American people have faced other grave crises in their history – with American courage, and with American resolution. They will do no less today.

They know the actualities of the attacks upon us. They know the necessities of a bold defense against these attacks. They know that the times call for clear heads and fearless hearts.

And with that inner strength that comes to a free people conscious of their duty, and conscious of the righteousness of what they do, they will – with Divine help and guidance – stand their ground against this latest assault upon their democracy, their sovereignty, and their freedom.

Document 12

"Repeal of Neutrality Act Means War"
Robert A. Taft
October 28, 1941

In keeping with his determination to pursue a policy of armed defense against Germany, President Franklin D. Roosevelt asked Congress to modify the neutrality laws to allow US merchant ships to arm themselves and enter the war zone. Senator Robert Taft (R-Ohio) objected to these changes in this address to the Senate. Congress nonetheless complied with Roosevelt's request in November.

Source: Senator Robert A. Taft (OH), "Repeal of Neutrality Act Means War," Congressional Record, part 8, 87: (October 28, 1941) p. S 8283–8284. https://goo.gl/PZU4eE.

... [T]he point I wanted to make is that the whole intention of the administration, every indication that a reasonable man can draw from its acts, is that it intends to go into war; and certainly, if we pass this resolution, and the administration has such an intention, we are going very shortly to become involved in war....

The power to declare war rests solely in the United States Congress. If the President can declare or create an undeclared naval war beyond our power to act upon, the Constitution might just as well be abolished. The Constitution deliberately gave to the representatives of the people the power to declare war, to pass on the question of war and peace, because that was something which kings had always done, which they had done against the interests of the people themselves, and which the founders of the Constitution thought the people ought to determine. It is true there have been one or two acts of war: but if Congress will refuse to repeal the Neutrality Act, I do not believe those acts of war can be continued. I do not believe the President is prepared to defy the express action of the Congress. Up to date he has not purported to do so. He has only claimed a power which I do not think he has. I stated on the floor of the Senate that I did not think he had the power to send American troops to Iceland, because Iceland was not in the Western Hemisphere, and it was already in the war zone. There was already there a British garrison. We have undertaken a joint defense of Iceland together with the British, who are actually at war with Germany. We can withdraw from Iceland. If we are sending convoys – as we are sending them – we can stop the policy of convoying vessels to Great Britain. . . .

Mr. Roosevelt says that our Navy has been instructed to shoot on sight.[1] There is no stated limitation on those orders. By what authority does Mr. Roosevelt send American youths to war – and that is what he is doing with the boys in the Navy – to prowl the ocean in quest of offensive warfare? Only Congress can constitutionally order our ships and our boys into an offensive war. Does Mr. Roosevelt contend, then, that he has assumed Hitlerian authority over the United States?

We have the President in effect admitting every charge made against him, that he was working toward war while promising peace, that he did intend to disregard Congress and the Constitution, and follow the course of dictatorship to an undeclared war.

There is just a shadow of substance to the claim that he can conduct war in defense of the United States. But defense has been stretched so thin that it cannot much longer be called anything like defense. We had first the defense of the United States. When we undertook a defense program, that is what everyone thought it meant, defense of continental United States, and the islands around it on this side of the Atlantic Ocean. . . .

Certainly the seizure of Iceland and Dakar is not defense of the United States.[2] It is an aggressive policy of defending the sea lanes to Great Britain. It is the defense of Great Britain, not of the United States.

The next position of the President was that we would shoot at any place where we found a German vessel in our defense waters. What our defense waters are he did not say. Apparently our defense waters extend to Iceland and well beyond. If we enact the pending measure, of course, our defense waters are going to be every ocean and every port in the entire world, in Asia, Africa, Europe, or Australia.

---

[1] See Document 11.

[2] Taft refers to the efforts of Great Britain and the Free French Forces to seize Dakar (in what is now Senegal) in September 1940. At the time, Dakar was part France's African colonial empire. Dakar had the best harbor in West Africa, stored French and Polish gold reserves, and was home to elements of the French fleet. These resources were now under control of the Vichy government, the French government the Germans allowed to operate in the southern part of France (so-called because its capital was the French city of Vichy).

The message on this measure finally contains the statement that we must fight in defense of American rights. Although we have seen fit to say that one of those rights, like the sending of our ships into belligerent ports, is a right we desire to give up, now the President says we should stand on that right, and precipitate the very kind of a conflict which brought on the World War....

We have to consider here the question whether we will approve a policy of undeclared naval war, whether we will give approval to the President, who has shown his desire to forward that war, who has constantly worked toward developing the war spirit in the United States, who apparently, under every reasonable conclusion from his speeches, is in favor of outright war – whether we shall vote here to authorize such a war....

Do we wish to keep our pledges to the people of the United States, pledges which practically every Senator here has made? There is no difference between the conditions of today and the conditions during the campaign of 1940. If anything, conditions today do not justify war as much as did conditions at that time. At that time Great Britain was being nightly bombarded, [and] the general feeling was that it might be successfully invaded at any moment. France had fallen. Hitler had spread over a great part of Europe, and it was obvious that he could spread over all the rest of Europe. There is no substantial difference between the conditions now and what the conditions were in 1940, when we gave our pledge. Possibly public opinion has changed, possibly it has not, but in the Senate we must decide this question on the basis of our own principles, and I say that no man who gave his pledge that we should keep out of war, who gave his pledge to do everything he could to keep the United States out of war, in November 1940 can today vote for the pending resolution without repudiating that pledge.[3]

---

[3] Taft refers perhaps to the pledge that Roosevelt made in 1940 that "your boys are not going to be sent into any foreign wars." Many candidates standing for Congress or Senate echoed the pledge. See Franklin D. Roosevelt, "Campaign Address at Boston Massachusetts, October 30, 1940," https://goo.gl/o22KWT.

Document 13

Gallup Polls
April – October 1941

These are examples of poll data Gallup collected to assess Americans' views about the European War between April and October of 1941. By this point, President Franklin D. Roosevelt had established his Lend-Lease policy. In September, in the wake of the Greer incident (Document 11), Roosevelt ordered U.S. ships to protect British convoys carrying American goods overseas and to shoot on sight any German submarines or ships discovered in American-controlled waters. In announcing each policy, Roosevelt asked for the nation's support. Gallup polled Americans to determine their reactions to these developments.

We have edited Gallup's presentation of the data he collected. On two occasions (the April 25 and October 8 polls), Gallup excluded the "no opinion" or "decline to respond" option when calculating the percentages for other possible responses. To avoid confusion, we provide the "no opinion" data for these two polls in footnotes.

Source: George H. Gallup, The Gallup Poll: Public Opinion 1935-1971, Vol. I: 1935-1948 (NY: Random House, 1972), p. 275, 276, 278, 299, and 301.

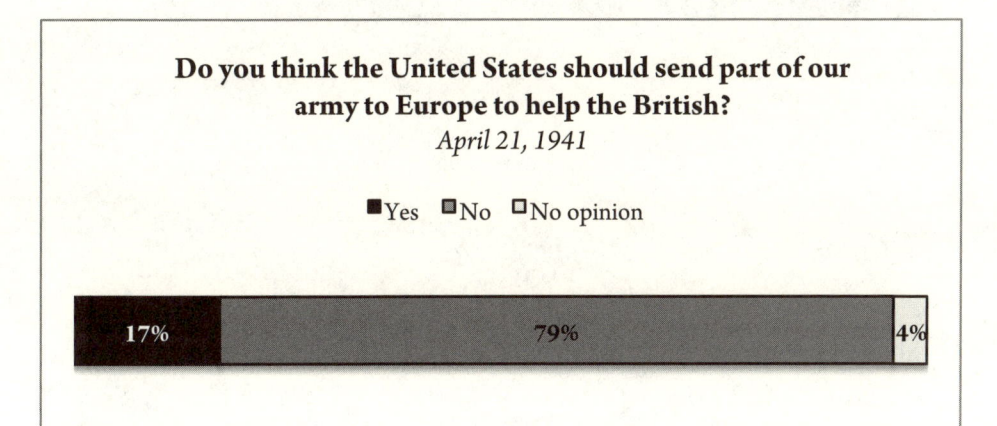

Do you think the United States should send part of our army to Europe to help the British?
April 21, 1941

■Yes ■No □No opinion

| 17% | 79% | 4% |

Do you think the United States should send part of our air force with American pilots to Europe to help the British?

April 21, 1941

■Yes ■No □No opinion

| 24% | 69% | 7% |

Do you think the United States should send part of our warships manned by American sailors to Europe to help the British?

April 21, 1941

■Yes ■No □No opinion

| 27% | 67% | 6% |

Should the United States Navy be used to guard ships carrying war materials to Britain?
April 23, 1941

■ Yes ■ No □ No opinion

Region	Yes	No	No opinion
National Response	41%	50%	9%
BY REGION			
New England	41%	49%	10%
Middle Atlantic	41%	49%	10%
East Central	35%	56%	9%
West Central	33%	58%	9%
South	59%	30%	11%
West	42%	52%	6%

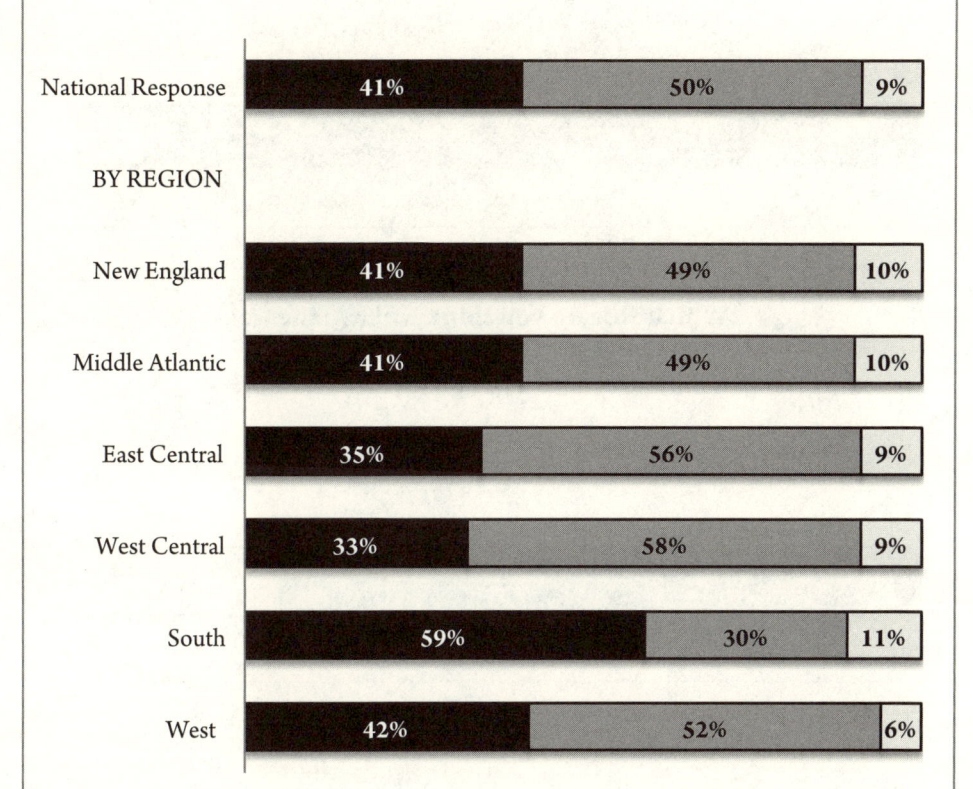

If it appears that Britain will be defeated unless we use part of our navy to protect ships going to Britain, would you favor or oppose such convoys?
April 23, 1941

■ Favor ■ Oppose □ No opinion

| 71% | 21% | 8% |

Which side do you think will win the war – Germany and Italy, or England?
April 25, 1941

■ Germany & Italy ■ England ■ Stalemate □ No opinion

| 11% | 57% | 8% | 24% |

Do you think Britain should try to get together with Germany to work out some sort of peace, or do you think Britain should go on fighting?[1]

April 25, 1941

■ Make peace   ■ Go on fighting

| 29% | 71% |

Do you think the United States will go into the war with Europe sometime before it's over, or do you think we will stay out of the war?

April 27, 1941

■ Will go in   ■ Will stay out

| 82% | 18% |

---

[1] Gallup reports that 9% of respondents had no opinion on this question. He excluded the "no opinion" responses before calculating the percentages for "Make peace" and "Go on fighting."

If you were asked to vote today on the question of the United States entering the war against Germany and Italy, how would you vote – to go into the war, or to stay out of the war?
April 28, 1941

■ Go in   ■ Stay out

| 19% | 81% |

If it appeared certain that there was no other way to defeat Germany and Italy except for the United States to go to war against them, would you be in favor of the United States going to war?
April 28, 1941

■ Yes   ■ No   □ No opinion

| 68% | 24% | 8% |

**Are you familiar with the views which
Charles Lindbergh has expressed concerning American
foreign policy?**
May 9, 1941

■ Yes ■ No

| 58% | 42% |

**Asked of those who responded in the affirmative:
Do you agree or disagree with what
Charles Lindbergh says?**
May 9, 1941

■ Agree ■ Disagree ☐ No opinion

| 24% | 63% | 13% |

If Canada is actually invaded by any European power, do you think the United States should use its army and navy to aid Canada?
May 10, 1941

■ Yes ■ No ☐ No opinion

Yes	No	No opinion
90%	5%	5%

Do you approve or disapprove of having the United States shoot at German submarines or warships on sight?
September 26, 1941

■ Approve ■ Disapprove ☐ No opinion

Approve	Disapprove	No opinion
56%	34%	10%

Should the Neutrality Act be changed to permit American merchant ships with American crews to carry war materials to Britain?
October 1, 1941

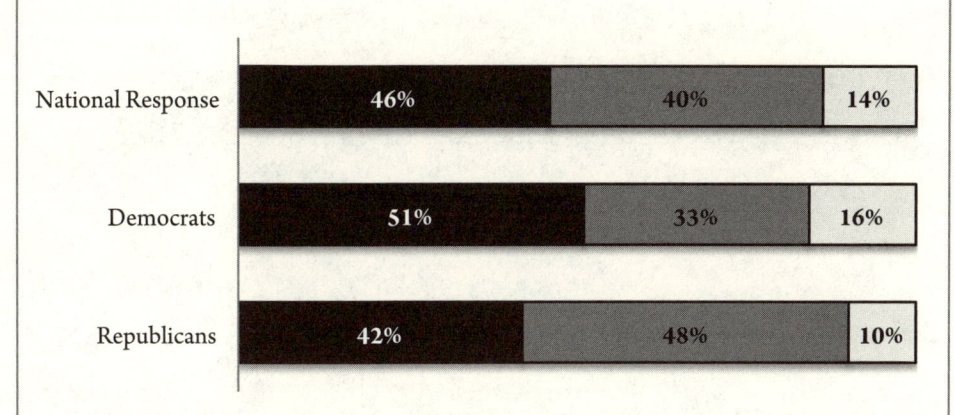

■ Yes ■ No □ No opinion

	Yes	No	No opinion
National Response	46%	40%	14%
Democrats	51%	33%	16%
Republicans	42%	48%	10%

In general, do you approve or disapprove of having the United States Navy shoot at German submarines or warships on sight?
October 3, 1941

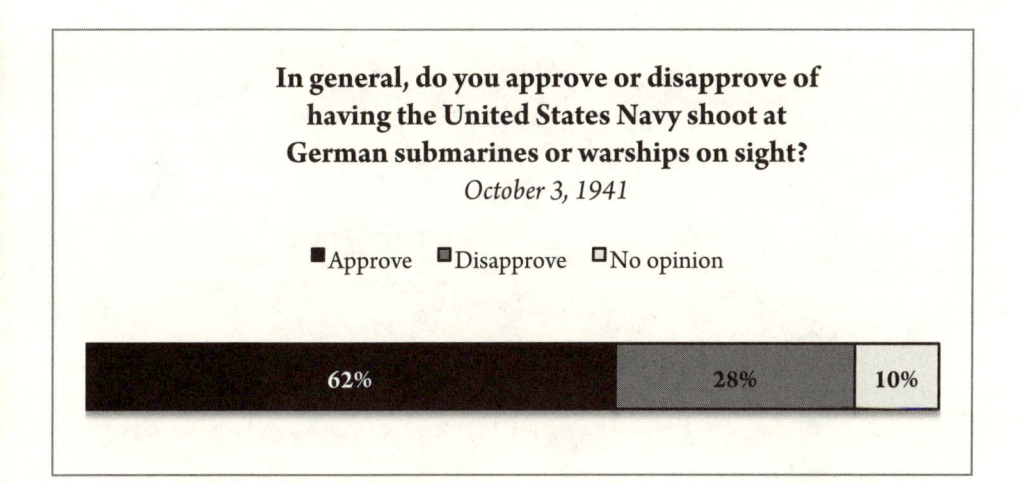

■ Approve ■ Disapprove □ No opinion

Approve	Disapprove	No opinion
62%	28%	10%

So far as you personally are concerned, do you think President Roosevelt has gone too far in his policies of helping Britain, or not far enough?[2]

October 8, 1941

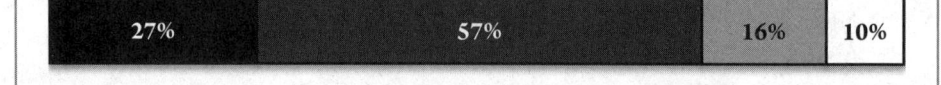

■ Too far ■ About right ■ Not far enough ◻ No opinion

| 27% | 57% | 16% | 10% |

---

[10] Ten percent of respondents had no opinion on this question. Gallup excluded the "no opinion" responses before calculating the percentages for the other possible responses.

Document 14

Reacting to Pearl Harbor
Claude R. Wickard
December 7, 1941

At 6 am on December 7, 1941, the Japanese launched two consecutive attacks on the American fleet stationed at Pearl Harbor on the island of Oahu, Hawaii. The Japanese sank or damaged 18 ships (including 8 battleships) and killed 2,405 Americans. Over the next 24 hours, the Japanese attacked British, Dutch, and American territories (including Guam and the Philippines) in Southeast Asia. In this diary excerpt, Secretary of Agriculture Claude R. Wickard recounted the president's conversation with his Cabinet officers and Congressional leaders after the attack on Pearl Harbor. It reveals the sense of confusion and misinformation in the hours after the attack.

Source: Claude R. Wickard Papers, Department of Agriculture Files: Cabinet Meetings, 1941-1942 (Box 13). https://goo.gl/EirzuB

At about four o'clock on the afternoon of December 7, I received a call from the White House saying that there would be a special meeting of the Cabinet in the President's study in the White House proper at 8:30 that evening. I had been writing all afternoon and Louise[1] had been busy so we had not listened to the radio, but I immediately concluded that the Japanese situation had taken a turn for the worse. Within a few minutes after the White House call we were able to get from radio reports that Honolulu and perhaps Manila had been attacked.[2] Later the announcers said that Manila had not been attacked but that three or four hundred lives had been lost in attacks in Hawaii.

The Cabinet members were ushered into the President's study at 8:40. Harry Hopkins was present.[3] The President began by saying that this was the

---

[1] Wickard's wife
[2] Japan invaded the Philippines on December 8, 1941.
[3] Harry Hopkins was a close advisor to FDR, chief architect of the New Deal, and an informal emissary to British Prime Minister Winston Churchill during World War II.

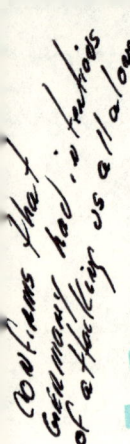

most important Cabinet meeting since 1861. He then told of the attack today in Hawaii. He said the attack was a serious one which he would describe later. He continued by saying that there was no question but that the Japanese had been told by the Germans a few weeks ago that they were winning the war and that they would soon dominate Africa as well as Europe. They were going to isolate England and were also going to completely dominate the situation in the Far East. The Japs had been told if they wanted to be cut in on the spoils they would have to come in the war now.

The President said that it would have been necessary to start making plans for today's attack at least three weeks ago. He then related how the Japanese Envoys, even today, had asked for a conference with Secretary Hull at the hour when the attack was being made in Hawaii.[4] He said that the Japanese had started a war [while] carrying on peace negotiations.

The President said that Guam and Wake Islands were also under attack.[5] He said these Islands were poorly fortified and that they would soon be in Japanese hands. He then read a message which he said he was going to read tomorrow at a joint session of Congress. He said that the message was subject to revision as later events might warrant. The message was short and merely stated how Japan had attacked while still carrying on peace negotiations. It ended by stating that he was asking Congress to declare that a state of war had existed since Japan's attack. He indicated that he did not know whether Japan had declared war or not. He also said there was a chance that the Germans would also declare war. There was considerable discussion of the proposed message. Secretary Hull said that he thought that there should be a complete statement on the events leading up to the attack. The President disagreed but Hull said he thought the most important war in 500 years deserved more than

---

[4] Cordell Hull was Secretary of State from 1933-1944.

[5] Located 2,496 miles due east of the Philippines, Guam is an island in the southwest Pacific. During the Spanish American War, the United States captured Guam, which from 1565 to the early nineteenth century had been an important base for Spanish ships traveling from Spanish Mexico to the Spanish Philippines. (Mexico gained its independence from Spain in 1821.) Following the war it became an American territory, which it remains. The Japanese captured Guam on December 7, 1941. The United States retook the island July 21, 1944. Wake Island is 1,500 miles east of Guam. The United States had taken possession of Wake in 1898, the same year it annexed the Hawaiian Islands and took Guam and the Philippines in the Spanish-American War. Naval facilities on the islands were part of the infrastructure through which the United States controlled the Pacific Ocean. The Japanese captured Wake on December 23, 1941 and held it until the end of the war.

Reacting to Pearl Harbor ← more "Proof" 77

a short statement. Secretary Stimson said that Germany had inspired and planned this whole affair and that the President should so state in his message.[6] The President disagreed with this suggestion.

The President went into the confidential reports of the attack which he said must be kept in strict secrecy. He first indicated that aircraft had been destroyed in large numbers in the attack. He then revealed that six out of seven of the battleships in Pearl Harbor had been damaged – very severely. I was shocked at the news; so were other members of the cabinet. The Secretary of the Navy lost his air of bravado.[7] Secretary Stimson was very sober.

The President said that the Japanese were hoping to bring about the transfer of American naval vessels from the Atlantic to the Pacific. He said he wanted to avoid this if [at] all possible. He said that he didn't want to tell Congressional leaders (of both parties – including Senators Barkley, Johnson, Austin and Connally, Speaker Rayburn, and Congressmen Jere Cooper, Martin, Bloom, and Doxey) who were waiting to come to his study all the things he had told us.[8]

When they came in he said that it was very unpleasant to be a War President and then he recounted the series of events leading up to the attacks of today. He said that he wanted to deliver a message to a joint session of Congress tomorrow. After a short discussion it was decided to have him address the session at 12:30. Some of the Congressmen wanted to know if he were going to ask for a declaration of war. The President said he didn't know yet what he was going to say because the events of the next fourteen hours would be numerous and all-important. The President revealed that at least battleships were damaged. This caused considerable consternation among the

---

[6] Henry L. Stimson was Secretary of War from 1940-1945.

[7] William Franklin "Frank" Knox was Secretary of the Navy from July 1940 until his death on April 28, 1944. A newspaper publisher, he was also the Republican nominee for Vice President in 1936. Because Knox supported aid to Britain, and Roosevelt wanted to create bi-partisan support for his defense policies, Roosevelt appointed Knox to his cabinet after the fall of France to the Nazi invasion. Although a forceful advocate for the war effort, Knox was not an active administrator. During his tenure, naval operations were handled for the most part by Chief of Naval Operations Ernest J. King and Assistant Secretary James Forrestal.

[8] Alben Barkley (D-Kentucky), who was Senate majority leader; Hiram Johnson (R-California); Warren Austin, (R-Vermont), who was assistant minority leader; Tom Connally, (D-Texas), who was chairman of the Senate Foreign Relations Committee; Sam Rayburn (D-Texas); Jere Cooper, (D-Tennessee); Joseph Martin, (R-Massachusetts), who was House minority leader; Sol Bloom, (D-New York), who was chairman of the House committee on foreign affairs; Wall Doxey (D-Mississippi).

Congressional leaders. Connally asked what damage we had inflicted on the Japs. The President indicated he didn't know but went on to say we had no information to indicate that we had severely damaged the Japs. Connolly exploded by saying: "Where were our forces – asleep? How can we go to war without anything to fight with?" The President told how the Germans might have been five hundred miles away at dark last night since they had twelve hours of sailing in the long darkness.

The President went on to say that the distance to Japan made it very difficult for us to attack Japan. He said that each thousand miles from base cut the efficiency of the Navy five percent. He pointed out that it would be necessary to strangle Japan rather than whip her and that it took longer. He once spoke about two or three years being required.

The meeting broke up about 10 o'clock. Everyone was very sober. The President began to dictate a statement for the press. Some of us stayed around for nearly an hour. I talked to the Vice President[9] who said many times that it was all for the best. I reminded him that he had made a similar statement when we were at the Convention at Chicago last year when it seemed that everything was crashing around us.[10]

Through it all the President was calm and deliberate. I could not help but admire his clear statements of the situation. He evidently realizes the seriousness of the situation and perhaps gets much comfort out of the fact that today's action will unite the American people. I don't know anybody in the United States who can come close to measuring up to his foresight and acumen in this critical hour.

As I drove home I could not refrain from wondering at the fates that caused me to be present at one of the most important conferences in the history of this nation.

---

[9] Henry Wallace
[10] Wickard may be referring here either to the controversy surrounding Roosevelt's nomination for an unprecedented third term or to the opposition that Wallace, who was viewed as having socialist sympathies, met as the Vice-Presidential nominee.

Document 7 Photo Illustration

First Lady Eleanor Roosevelt and pilot Charles Alfred Anderson, April 1941 (*National Air and Space Museum, Smithsonian Institution, SI Neg. No 90-7010*).

Document 17 Photo Illustration
Photo 1

WESTERN DEFENSE COMMAND AND FOURTH ARMY
WARTIME CIVIL CONTROL ADMINISTRATION

Presidio of San Francisco, California
May 3, 1942

INSTRUCTIONS
TO ALL PERSONS OF
JAPANESE
ANCESTRY

Living in the Following Area:

All of that portion of the City of Los Angeles, State of California, within that boundary beginning at the point at which North Figueroa Street meets a line following the middle of the Los Angeles River; thence southerly and following the said line to East First Street ; thence westerly on East First Street to Alameda Street ; thence southerly on Alameda Street to East Third Street; thence northwesterly on East Third Street to Main Street; thence northerly on Main Street to First Street; thence northwesterly on First Street to Figueroa Street; thence northeasterly on Figueroa Street to the point of beginning.

Pursuant to the provisions of Civilian Exclusion Order No. 33, this Headquarters, dated May 3, 1942, all persons of Japanese ancestry, both alien and non-alien, will be evacuated from the above area by 12 o'clock noon, P. W . T., Saturday, May 9, 1942.

No Japanese person living in the above area will be permitted to change residence after 12 o'clock noon, P.W.T., Sunday, May 3, 1942, without obtaining special permission from the representative of the Commanding General, Southern California Sector, at the Civil Control Station located at:
>Japanese Union Church,
>120 North San Pedro Street,
>Los Angeles, California.

Such permits will only be granted for the purpose of uniting members of a family, or in cases of grave emergency.

The Civil Control Station is equipped to assist the Japanese Population affected by this evacuation in the following ways:

1. Give advice and instructions on the evacuation.
2. Provide services with respect to the management, leasing, sale, storage or other disposition of most kinds of property, such as real estate, business and professional equipment, household goods, boats, automobiles and livestock.
3. Provide temporary residence elsewhere for all Japanese in family groups.
4. Transport persons and a limited amount of clothing and equipment to their new residence.

The Following Instructions Must Be Observed:
1. A responsible member of each family, preferably the head of the family, or the person in whose name

most of the property is held, and each individual living alone, will report to the Civil Control Station to receive further instructions. This must be done between 8:00 A. M. and 5:00 P. M. on Monday, May 4, 1942, or between 8:00 A. M. and 5:00 P. M. on Tuesday, May 5, 1942.

    2. Evacuees must carry with them on departure for the Assembly Center, the following property:
- (a) Bedding and linens (no mattress) for each member of the family;
- (b) Toilet articles for each member of the family;
- (c) Extra clothing for each member of the family;
- (d) Sufficient knives, forks, spoons, plates, bowls and cups for each member of the family;
- (e) Essential personal effects for each member of the family.

    All items carried will be securely packaged, tied and plainly marked with the name of the owner and numbered in accordance with instructions obtained at the Civil Control Station. The size and number of the packages is limited to that which can be carried by the individual or family group.

    3. No pets of any kind will be permitted.

    4. No personal items and no household goods will be shipped to the Assembly Center.

    5. The United States Government through its agencies will provide for the storage, at the sole risk of the owner, of the more substantial household items, such as iceboxes, washing machines, pianos and other heavy furniture. Cooking utensils and other small items will be accepted for storage if crated, packed and plainly marked with the name and address of the owner. Only one name and address will be used by a given family.

    6. Each family, and individual living alone, will be furnished transportation to the Assembly Center or will be authorized to travel by private automobile in a supervised group. All instructions pertaining to the movement will be obtained at the Civil Control Station.

Go to the Civil Control Station between the hours of 8:00 A. M. and 5:00 P. M., Monday, May 4, 1942, or between the hours of 8:00 A. M. and 5:00 P. M., Tuesday, May 5, 1942, to receive further instructions.

J.L DeWITT
Lieutenant General, U. S. Army
Commanding

SEE CIVILIAN EXCLUSION ORDER NO. 33.

"Instructions to Persons of Japanese Ancestry, Presidio of San Francisco, California, May 3, 1942." (Box 74, Item 33, Manzanar War Relocation Center Records [Collection 122], Department of Special Collections, Young Research Library, University of California, Los Angeles. Available from UCLA Institute on Primary Resources, https://goo.gl/crkBAP).

Document 17 Photo Illustration
Photo 2

"Civilian exclusion order #5, posted at First and Front streets, directing removal by April 7 of persons of Japanese ancestry, from the first San Francisco section to be affected by evacuation." *Dorothea Lange, April 1942, from a group of photos on the evacuation and relocation of Japanese Americans living in California during World War II (Library of Congress, Farm Security Administration and Office of War Information Collection, LC-USZ62- 34565).*

Document 17 Photo Illustration
Photo 3

A young San Francisco resident waits for the bus that will carry him and other Japanese Americans to a relocation center. *Dorothea Lange, April 1942 (Library of Congress, LC-USZ62- 17132).*

Document 25 Photo Illustration

Troops exiting an amphibious landing vehicle and wading onto a Normandy beach *("Into the Jaws of Death – U.S. Troops wading through water and Nazi gunfire," June 6, 1944," Public Domain Photographs, 1882-1962, Franklin D. Roosevelt Library).*

Document 27 Photo Illustration
Photo 1

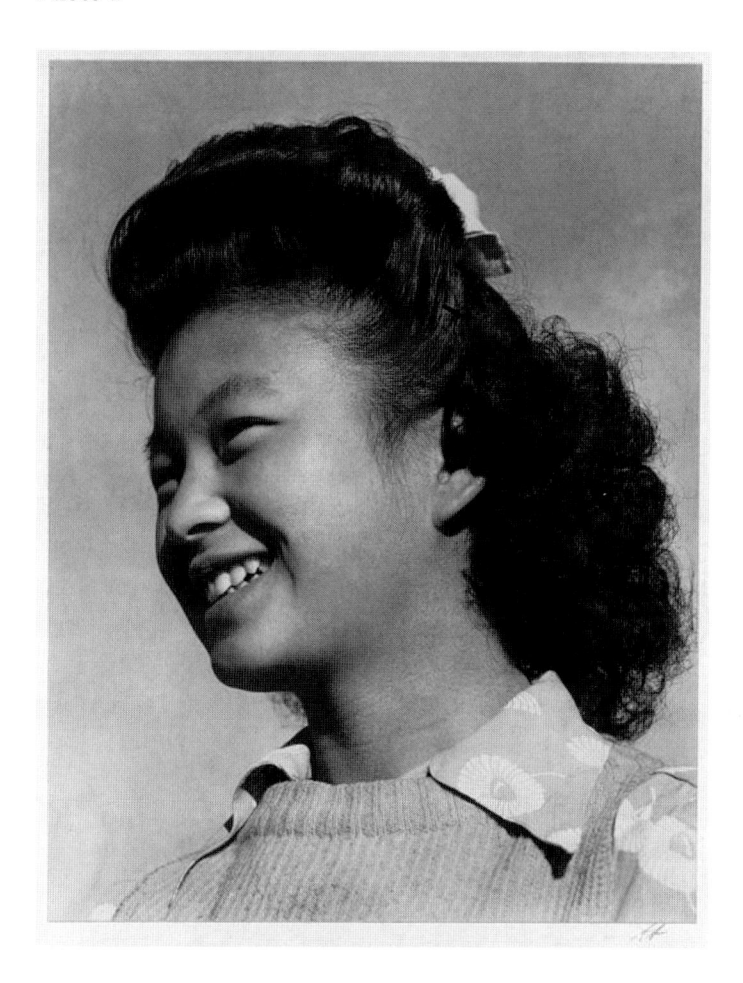

"Americanism is a matter of the mind and heart." *Ansel Adams, photograph of Yeko Yamamoto, little girl, Manzanar Relocation Center, 1943 (Library of Congress, LC-DIG- ppprs-00434).*

Document 27 Photo Illustration
Photos 2 and 3

Photo 2: "One son of the Yonemitsu Family is an X-ray technician in the Manzanar Hospital." *Ansel Adams, photograph of Michael Yonemetsu, [i.e., Yonemitsu] x-ray specialist, Manzanar Relocation Center, California (Library of Congress, LC-DIG- ppprs-00254).*

Photo 3: "Another son is in the U. S. Army." *Ansel Adams, Pictures and mementoes on phonograph top: Yonemitsu home, Manzanar Relocation Center, 1943. (Library of Congress, LC-DIG-ppprs-00278).*

Document 15

"A Date Which Will Live in Infamy"
Franklin D. Roosevelt
December 8, 1941

The day after the Japanese attack on Pearl Harbor, President Franklin D. Roosevelt delivered this Address to a Joint Session of Congress. The address was broadcast live on radio to the American people. An hour after he finished, Congress declared war on Japan. Germany and Italy declared war on the United States on December 11, 1941. The United States was now fighting a two-front world war.

Source: "Joint Address to Congress Leading to a Declaration of War Against Japan (1941)," in 100 Milestone Documents, *an online library compiled by the "Our Documents" Initiative, a cooperative effort of the National Archives and Records Administration with National History Day and USA Freedom Corps.* https://goo.gl/PaEF1b

---

Mr. Vice President, and Mr. Speaker, and Members of the Senate and House of Representatives:

Yesterday, December 7, 1941 – a date which will live in infamy – the United States of America was suddenly and deliberately attacked by naval and air forces of the Empire of Japan.

The United States was at peace with that Nation and, at the solicitation of Japan, was still in conversation with its Government and its Emperor looking toward the maintenance of peace in the Pacific. Indeed, one hour after Japanese air squadrons had commenced bombing in the American Island of Oahu, the Japanese Ambassador to the United States and his colleague delivered to our Secretary of State a formal reply to a recent American message. And while this reply stated that it seemed useless to continue the existing diplomatic negotiations, it contained no threat or hint of war or of armed attack.

It will be recorded that the distance of Hawaii from Japan makes it obvious that the attack was deliberately planned many days or even weeks ago. During the intervening time the Japanese Government has deliberately sought to deceive the United States by false statements and expressions of hope for continued peace.

The attack yesterday on the Hawaiian Islands has caused severe damage to American naval and military forces. I regret to tell you that very many American lives have been lost. In addition American ships have been reported torpedoed on the high seas between San Francisco and Honolulu.

Yesterday the Japanese Government also launched an attack against Malaya.

Last night Japanese forces attacked Hong Kong.

Last night Japanese forces attacked Guam.

Last night Japanese forces attacked the Philippine Islands.

Last night the Japanese attacked Wake Island. And this morning the Japanese attacked Midway Island.

Japan has, therefore, undertaken a surprise offensive extending throughout the Pacific area. The facts of yesterday and today speak for themselves. The people of the United States have already formed their opinions and well understand the implications to the very life and safety of our Nation.

As Commander in Chief of the Army and Navy I have directed that all measures be taken for our defense.

But always will our whole Nation remember the character of the onslaught against us.

No matter how long it may take us to overcome this premeditated invasion, the American people in their righteous might will win through to absolute victory. I believe that I interpret the will of the Congress and of the people when I assert that we will not only defend ourselves to the uttermost but will make it very certain that this form of treachery shall never again endanger us.

Hostilities exist. There is no blinking at the fact that our people, our territory, and our interests are in grave danger.

With confidence in our armed forces – with the unbounding determination of our people – we will gain the inevitable triumph – so help us God.

I ask that the Congress declare that since the unprovoked and dastardly attack by Japan on Sunday, December 7, 1941, a state of war has existed between the United States and the Japanese Empire.

Document 16

Executive Order No. 9066 – Resulting in the Relocation of Japanese

Franklin D. Roosevelt
February 19, 1942

Bowing to political pressure, President Franklin D. Roosevelt issued Executive Order No. 9066 allowing military commanders to declare areas off-limits to "any or all persons." Public Law 503 made violation of military orders issued under the authority of EO 9066 a federal offense. Congress approved the law unanimously, and Roosevelt signed it. General John L. Dewitt was in charge of the Western Command that included California, Oregon, and Washington. "A Jap's a Jap. It makes no difference whether the Jap is a citizen or not," he said. He immediately excluded any persons of Japanese ancestry, citizen and non-citizen, from residence in the Western Command. Some Japanese-Americans refused to comply, and their convictions became the basis for court challenges on the constitutionality of exclusion and internment that went up to the Supreme Court (Document 29). EO 9066 was the basis for the removal and internment of Japanese Americans (Documents 17 and 27).

Source: **100 Milestone Documents,** *an online library compiled by the "Our Documents" Initiative, a cooperative effort of the National Archives and Records Administration with National History Day and USA Freedom Corps.* https://goo.gl/JjrUC8

The President
Executive Order
Authorizing the Secretary of War to Prescribe Military Areas

Whereas the successful prosecution of the war requires every possible protection against espionage and against sabotage to national-defense material, national-defense premises, and national-defense utilities as defined in Section 4, Act of April 20, 1918, 40 Stat. 533, as amended by the Act of November 30,

1940, 54 Stat. 1220, and the Act of August 21, 1941, 55 Stat. 655 (U.S.C., Title 50, Sec. 104);

Now, therefore, by virtue of the authority vested in me as President of the United States, and Commander in Chief of the Army and Navy, I hereby authorize and direct the Secretary of War, and the Military Commanders whom he may from time to time designate, whenever he or any designated Commander deems such action necessary or desirable, to prescribe military areas in such places and of such extent as he or the appropriate Military Commander may determine, from which any or all persons may be excluded, and with respect to which, the right of any person to enter, remain in, or leave shall be subject to whatever restrictions the Secretary of War or the appropriate Military Commander may impose in his discretion. The Secretary of War is hereby authorized to provide for residents of any such area who are excluded therefrom, such transportation, food, shelter, and other accommodations as may be necessary, in the judgment of the Secretary of War or the said Military Commander, and until other arrangements are made, to accomplish the purpose of this order. The designation of military areas in any region or locality shall supersede designations of prohibited and restricted areas by the Attorney General under the Proclamations of December 7 and 8, 1941,[1] and shall supersede the responsibility and authority of the Attorney General under the said Proclamations in respect of such prohibited and restricted areas.

I hereby further authorize and direct the Secretary of War and the said Military Commanders to take such other steps as he or the appropriate Military Commander may deem advisable to enforce compliance with the restrictions applicable to each Military area hereinabove authorized to be designated, including the use of Federal troops and other Federal Agencies, with authority to accept assistance of state and local agencies.

I hereby further authorize and direct all Executive Departments, independent establishments and other Federal Agencies, to assist the Secretary of War or the said Military Commanders in carrying out this Executive Order, including the furnishing of medical aid, hospitalization, food, clothing, transportation, use of land, shelter, and other supplies, equipment, utilities, facilities, and services.

This order shall not be construed as modifying or limiting in any way the authority heretofore granted under Executive Order No. 8972, dated

---

[1] These proclamations dealt with restricting the activities of enemy aliens, that is, German and Japanese citizens living in the United States.

December 12, 1941,[2] nor shall it be construed as limiting or modifying the duty and responsibility of the Federal Bureau of Investigation, with respect to the investigation of alleged acts of sabotage or the duty and responsibility of the Attorney General and the Department of Justice under the Proclamations of December 7 and 8, 1941, prescribing regulations for the conduct and control of alien enemies, except as such duty and responsibility is superseded by the designation of military areas hereunder.

Franklin D. Roosevelt

---

[2] This Executive Order allowed the Secretary of War and the Secretary of the Navy to establish guards and patrols and to take other measures to protect national defense materials and premises.

Document 17

Japanese American Evacuation
April – May 1942

In March 1942, President Franklin D. Roosevelt established the War Relocation Authority to manage the forced removal of persons of Japanese ancestry from the West Coast. Approximately 72,000 Japanese-Americans and 38,000 Japanese immigrants were sent to 10 internment camps located throughout interior areas of western states. Pages 80-81 reproduce the evacuation order as it was posted in west coast communities. The photo on page 82, taken by photographer Dorothea Lange, shows how the poster appeared at one San Francisco location. The War Relocation Authority hired photographer Dorothea Lange to document the removal process as humane and efficient. Lange took the assignment even though she disagreed with the decision to intern American citizens, and tried to capture the confusion and anxiety of the evacuees (see photo 3 on page 83). She hoped that her photographs would encourage people to think twice, but the majority of her photographs were censored and never published during the war.

Source: For the poster – "Instructions to Persons of Japanese Ancestry, Presidio of San Francisco, California, May 3, 1942." (Box 74, Item 33, Manzanar War Relocation Center Records [Collection 122], Department of Special Collections, Young Research Library, University of California, Los Angeles. Available from UCLA Institute on Primary Resources, https://goo.gl/gTN9Tg).

For the photo – Dorothea Lange, "Civilian exclusion order #5, posted at First and Front streets, directing removal by April 7 of persons of Japanese ancestry, from the first San Francisco section to be affected by evacuation," April 1942, Prints and Photographs Division, Library of Congress (93) LC-USZ62-34565.

Document 18

First News of the Final Solution
August 10 – 11, 1942

In August 1942, Gerhart Riegner, the Geneva-based representative for the World Jewish Congress, came to the U.S. Consulate in Switzerland and told Vice-Consul Howard Elting, Jr. disturbing news of a German plan to exterminate Europe's Jews. While passing this information onto the State Department, Elting and Leland Harrison, the U.S. Minister to Switzerland, each separately commented on the report's reliability. It took until November 24, 1942 for the U.S. and British government to publically confirm that the report was correct.

On December 17, the United States, as part of a joint statement from the Allied nations, denounced Germany's plan to exterminate the Jews of Europe and vowed to punish those responsible. Nonetheless, details about the murder of Europe's Jews received little press attention during the war and many Americans were shocked to discover the truth when Allied troops entered the concentration and extermination camps in 1944–45.

Source: U.S. State Department receives information from Switzerland regarding the Nazi plan to murder the Jews of Europe, "America and the Holocaust," The American Experience, produced by WGBH, Boston. https://goo.gl/G7mn4v. See also Michael Neufeld and Michael Berenbaum, The Bombing of Auschwitz: Should the Allies Have Attempted It? (New York: St. Martin's Press, published in association with the United States Holocaust Memorial Museum, 2000), 76 – 79.

Harrison to the State Department

STRICTLY CONFIDENTIAL.

Gerhardt M. Riegner Secretary World Jewish Congress Geneva called on Vice Consul Elting Geneva Saturday eighth greatly agitated and requested following quoted message be transmitted for information American and other Allied Governments and be notified in Department's discretion to Dr Stephen Wise New York City:

"Informer reported to have close connections with highest German authorities who has previously generally reliable reports says that in Fuehrer's [sic] headquarters plan under consideration to exterminate at one blow this fall three and half to four millions Jews following deportation from countries occupied, controlled by Germany and concentration in east. Method execution undecided but prussic acid[1] has been considered. Information transmitted with reservation as exactitude cannot be ascertained."

CONFIDENTIAL Legation[2] note: Legation has no information which would tend to confirm this report which is however forwarded in accordance with Riegner's wishes. In conversation with Elting Riegner drew attention to recently reported Jewish deportations eastward from occupied France, protectorate and probably elsewhere. The report has earmarks of war rumor inspired by fear and what is commonly understood to be the actually miserable condition of these refugees who face decimation as result physical maltreatment persecution and scarcely endurable privations malnutrition and disease.

HARRISON

Elting to the State Department

MEMORANDUM
Subject: Conversation with Mr. Gerhart M. RIEGNER, Secretary of World Jewish Congress

This morning Mr. Gerhart M. RIEGNER, Secretary of the World Jewish Congress in Geneva, called in great agitation. He stated that he had just received a report from a German business man of considerable prominence,[3] who is said to have excellent political and military connections in Germany and from whom reliable and important political information has been obtained on two previous occasions, to the effect that there has been and is being considered in Hitler's headquarters a plan to exterminate all Jews from Germany and German controlled areas in Europe after they have been

---

[1] Zyklon B, the gas used in the gas chambers, was derived from prussic acid.
[2] By "legation," Harrison means the staff of the American diplomatic mission in Switzerland.
[3] Riegner's informant was Eduard Schulte, a leading German industrialist who served as an Allied spy throughout the war.

concentrated in the east (presumably Poland). The number involved is said to be between three-and-a-half and four millions and the object is to permanently settle the Jewish question in Europe. The mass execution if decided upon would allegedly take place this fall.

Riegner stated that according to his informant the use of prussic acid was mentioned as a means of accomplishing the executions. When I mentioned that this report seemed fantastic to me, Riegner said that it struck him in the same way but that from the fact that mass deportation had been taking place since July 16 as confirmed by reports received by him from Paris, Holland, Berlin, Vienna, and Prague it was always conceivable that such a diabolical plan was actually being considered by Hitler as a corollary.

According to Riegner, 14,000 Jews have already been deported from occupied France and 10,000 more are to be handed over from occupied France in the course of the next few days. Similarly from German sources 56,000 Jews have already been deported from the Protectorate together with unspecified numbers from Germany and other occupied countries.

Riegner said this report was so serious and alarming that he felt it his duty to make the following requests: (1) that the American and other Allied Governments be informed with regard thereto at once; (2) that they be asked to try by every means to obtain confirmation or denial; (3) that Dr. Stephen Wise, the president of his organization, be informed of the report.

I told Riegner that the information would be passed on to the Legation at once but that I was not in a position to inform him as to what action, if any, the Legation might take. He hoped that he might be informed in due course that the information had been transmitted to Washington.

For what it is worth, my personal opinion is that Riegner is a serious and balanced individual and that he would never have come to the Consulate with the above report if he had not had confidence in his informant's reliability and if he did not seriously consider that the report might well contain an element of truth. Again it is my opinion that the report should be passed on to the Department for what it is worth.

There is attached a draft of a telegram prepared by Riegner giving in his own words a telegraphic summary of his statements to me.

Howard Elting, Jr.
American Vice Consul

American Consulate
Geneva, Switzerland

Document 19

Pacific War Diary
James J. Fahey
1942 - 1945

James J. Fahey (1918–1991) became a literary celebrity in 1963 when he published the secret wartime diary that he had kept from October 1942 to December 1945. Fahey wrote graphically about the brutality of the naval war in the Pacific while serving as a seaman first class on the USS Montpelier. *He worked as a garbage man until he retired, and donated the profits from his book to charity.*

Source: Excerpts from Pacific War Diary, 1942–1945 *by James J. Fahey (New York: Houghton Mifflin, 1963). Copyright renewed 1991 by James J. Fahey. Used by permission of Houghton Mifflin Company. All rights reserved. Excerpts available from: https://goo.gl/APyYvR.*

November 23, 1942

It was a great feeling as I staggered up the gangway to the ship with my sea bag in one hand and the mattress cover loaded with blankets, mattresses, etc., over my shoulder. At last I have a home – and a warship at that.

January 26, 1943
New Hebrides

Last night they said we were about 2 ½ hours from the Jap fleet, but let them come. I came out here to see action and I hope this is the biggest battle of all time and it is also an honor to be on the flagship so I think this baby will give a good account of itself. Most of the crew would rather keep on going and see action than go back to the States. As for me, I would not trade my place with anyone back in the states. I do not know how I will feel when we run into action, but right now I feel in the pink of condition and don't care how many Japs I run into.

February 19, 1943

The press news said that our forces have complete control of Guadalcanal. Everyone was very happy to hear this. This is number one in the long climb up the Solomons that faces us. One of the fellows was electrocuted when he accidentally touched a live wire. We had church services for him, and his body was lowered over the side.

June 30, 1943

The Solomons are over five hundred miles long and most of the islands are Jap-held fortresses.... Our job will be to bombard the Japs on shore and prevent Jap subs and warships from attacking our transports, minelayers and troops.... Our bombardment will take place in darkness as usual right in the Japs' backyard. It will be a bad place to get hit because if you land in the water the sharks will get you, and if you land on one of the islands the Japs will get you and of course that means torture and death.

July 15, 1943

A big LST pulled alongside today ... [with] close to 300 wounded troops from Munda.... A lot of the wounded were cut very badly by Japanese knives...[1] Fighting the Japs is like fighting a wild animal. The troops said the Jap is not afraid to die, it is an honor to die for the Emperor, he is their God. A lot of the fighting is done at night and you can smell the Japs 25 yards away.... The Japs watch from coconut trees in the daytime and then when it becomes dark they sneak into your foxhole and cut your throat or throw in a hand grenade.... The Japs take all kinds of chances, they love to die. Our troops are advancing very slowly. It is a savage campaign.... You also hear all sorts of noises made by animals and you think it is the Japs. This is too much for some men and they crack up....

---

[1] An LST, or "landing ship, tank" was a military cargo ship used to transport men and materiel for amphibious landings.

October 19, 1943
Sidney, Australia

    It was quite a feeling to be back in civilization for the first time in almost a year. It was just as if we were coming home. A feeling came over us that we could not explain. It seemed like paradise. . . . This was the first time in over 10 months for some of the men to leave the ship and put their feet on land. . . .

    When you leave the ship you go through a beautiful park to get to the business section of Sidney. . . . The first thing that catches your eye are all the beautiful girls. The place is full of them. There are supposed to be 5 girls to every man but I think there are even more than that. Everyone is so friendly down here. I never saw such friendly people. The girls in the states could really learn something from the girls here. They treat you as if you were related and invite you home to meet the family. . . .

    We did not like to leave. When you know it's your last night in civilization you could walk on the soil all night, and just breathe the fresh air. It feels so good. You know it will be some time before you put your feet on anything like this again. . . . It is an experience you will never forget. You will put Australia down as the best liberty port in the world.

November 10, 1943

    This afternoon, while we were south of Bougainville . . . we came across a raft with four live Japs in it. . . . As the destroyer Spence came close to the raft, the Japs opened up with a machine gun at the destroyer. The Jap officer then put the gun in each man's mouth and fired, blowing out the back of each man's skull. One of the Japs did not want to die for the Emperor and put up a struggle. The others held him down. The officer was the last to die. He also blew his brains out. The Spence went in to investigate. All the bodies had disappeared into the water. There was nothing left but blood and an empty raft. Swarms of sharks were everywhere. The sharks ate well today. . . . We went to battle stations . . . and at 10PM we were attacked by enemy planes. . . . Later darkness descended and the rains came. . . .

June 4, 1944
(en route to the Mariana Islands[2] and the Invasion of Saipan, Guam, etc.)

Captain Hoffman spoke to the crew and said . . . it will be the largest [invasion] of the Pacific war. . . . While on watch I told Edgerton, Tojo Bonnette and the rest of the crew that I might sound crazy for saying such a thing but if I had my choice of leaving now for the states, that I would turn it down rather than miss this big invasion. I would not want to miss this for anything, and they felt the same way. I might be scared stiff before it was over, but I want to be there. I think that is the way most of the crew feels. It gets into your blood, after you have been down here a long time, you want to get into all the campaigns, you do not want to miss any.

June 6, 1944

At 6:30 PM this evening, the announcement came over the loudspeaker that the Allies landed in France. Everyone gave a big cheer when they heard this. I won $40 from the boys because some time ago I bet the invasion would come off about the middle of June. The air is a lot fresher now. Since we crossed the equator it is not so hot and sultry. . . .

June 20, 1944 *(the Battle of the Marianas, also called the Battle of the Philippine Sea)*

At 4 PM this afternoon we got the good news we have been waiting for, they finally know where the Jap fleet is, they said it's heading for the Philippines.[3] Our carrier planes picked them up this afternoon, everyone was glad to hear this. The Jap fleet is running away from us and heading to their base. We picked up speed and are after them. This news has put new life into the men. It is getting late and our only hope of doing any damage to them is to send our planes after them. Some of the men on this mission will not return, the Japs will give them a hot reception. It was 4:30PM when our [300] planes

---

[2] The Mariana Islands are a chain of islands approximately 2,000 miles southeast of Japan. Their capture from the Japanese was part of the American "island hopping" strategy undertaken to bring American bombers within range of Japan and, ultimately, to prepare for the invasion of Japan.

[3] The Japanese invaded the Philippines immediately following the attack on Pearl Harbor and occupied it until 1945, when American forces reestablished control.

took off.... The time dragged as we waited to hear from our pilots, everyone kept his fingers crossed, hoping for the best. It was like waiting in the death house for a pardon, and then it happened.

About 6:50PM word came that our pilots had caught up with the Jap navy and it said three carriers were damaged.... At about 9PM tonight our planes were returning. It was dark and they would have a tough job landing on the carriers, they were low on fuel and some were damaged, many had to make forced landings in the water. Then something never done before in war time happened, all the ships in this huge fleet put their lights on, and flares were dropped into the water. This all happened right in the Japs' back yard maybe 700 or 800 miles from the coast of Japan. We would be easy targets for Jap subs that might be around. It was a great decision to make and everyone thought the world of Admiral Marc Mitscher for doing this.

This would make it easier for our pilots to land, and if they did hit the water, they could be saved.... It was a shame to see our planes hitting the water. I saw one pilot on the wing of his plane waving his shirt.... A Jap plane also tried to land on one of our carriers.... It was quite a sight to see all the ships lit up, flares and rafts in the water and some planes crashing into the water, pilots and crews also in the water. You could see the planes circle and then land on the carriers.... The Japs would never do anything like this.

June 25, 1944

We got very close to Saipan today, some of our ships are still bombarding the Japs and our planes are doing a job on the troops. Most of the Japs are crowded up north on Saipan. It was funny to see some of the fellows fishing from the side of the ship, others laying in the sun getting a tan, and up forward on the bow some of the officers are boxing, while on the beach men are killing each other, some are in agony from wounds. Our planes are strafing and bombing and our ships are bombarding the Japs. The two scenes are so close to each other and yet it is from one extreme to another or two different worlds.

June 26, 1944 *(off Saipan while the battle rages on shore)*

I was talking to one of the men from the ammunition ship who was on the beach and he said some of the Japs are up in caves with big steel doors. They open a slide and fire at our troops and then close them. Our troops sneaked up on the Japs and when they opened the steel door they put a flamethrower in and wiped out the Japs. The bodies smelled when the flamethrowers hit them and the smell of burnt flesh is very strong. He said 1500 of our troops were killed the day before yesterday.

July 3, 1944

It will be quite a treat for us when we return home and go to sleep in a bed with nothing to spoil our sleep. It is just the little things in life that you look forward to when you go home. When you had them you thought nothing of them, you took them for granted. Now you look forward to meeting your family and friends, being able to go the corner store and get the morning paper, and read your favorite topics, or visit the drugstore for a big ice cream soda, looking at buildings and going to the Parish Church, and the local theater. Eating plenty of good food. You want to be free again and do what you want to do and go where you want to go, without someone always ordering you around. You want freedom.

November 17, 1944

The Captain spoke this evening and said we would pull into Ulithi[4] early Tues. morning. He also said the Japs are sending suicide planes against our ships in larger numbers now, they crash their planes against our ships, the pilot stays in the plane also. The Japs did this before but on a small scale. A suicide plane with its bombs can do a lot of damage when it hits a ship, you have to destroy it before it reaches you.

November 27, 1944
(*Account of 2 hour-long attack by 70 Kamikazes near Leyte, Philippines*)

At 10:50 AM this morning, General Quarters[5] sounded, all hands went to their battle stations. . . . It was not long after that when a force of about 30 Jap planes attacked us. Dive bombers and torpedo planes. . . . They had only one thing in mind and that was to crash into our ships, bombs and all. You have to blow them up, to damage them doesn't mean much. . . . A Jap plane came in on a battleship with its guns blazing away. Other Jap planes came in strafing one

---

[4] An atoll in the Caroline islands in the western Pacific, 850 miles east of the Philippines and 1,300 miles south of Japan.
[5] An announcement that everyone on ship must go to his battle station.

ship, dropping their bombs on another and crashing into another ship. The Jap planes were falling all around us....

One suicide dive bomber was heading right for us while we were firing at other attacking planes and if the 40mm mount behind us on the port side did not blow the Jap wing off, it would have killed all of us. When the wing was blown off it, the plane turned some and bounced off into the water and the bombs blew part of the plane onto our ship.... A Jap dive bomber crashed into one of the 40mm mounts ... parts of the plane flew everywhere.... Part of the motor hit Tomlinson, he had chunks of it all over him, his stomach, back, legs, etc. The rest of the crew were wounded, most of them were sprayed with gasoline from the plane.... The explosions were terrific as the suicide planes exploded in the water not too far away from our ship.... The water looked like it was on fire. It would have been curtains for us if they had crashed into us....

... It is a tough job to hold back this tidal wave of suicide planes. They come at you from all directions and also straight down at us at a very fast pace and some of the men have time for a few fast jokes, "This would be a great time to run out of ammunition." "This is mass suicide at its best."... How long will our luck hold out? ...

November 27, 1944, continued
(*Gory details of aftermath of the Kamikaze attack*)

Planes were falling all around us, bombs were coming too close for comfort. The Jap planes were cutting up the water with machine gun fire. All the guns on the ship were blazing away, talk about action, never a dull moment. The fellows were passing ammunition like lightening as the guns were turning in all directions spitting out hot steel. Parts of destroyed suicide planes were scattered all over the ship. During a lull in the action, the men would look around for Jap souvenirs.... I got part of the plane. The deck near my [machine gun] mount was covered with blood, guts, brains, tongues, scalps, hearts, arms, etc. from the Jap pilots. One of the Marines cut the ring off the finger of one of the dead pilots. They had to put the hose on to wash the blood off the deck. The deck ran with blood. The Japs were spattered all over the place. One of the fellows had a Jap scalp, it looked just like you skinned an animal....

These suicide or kamikaze pilots wanted to destroy us, our ships, and themselves. This gives you an idea of what kind of enemy we are fighting.

Pacific War Diary

January 1, 1945

Happy New Year. Today is the first day of 1945. . . . It is just another day out here. I think the war will be over this year. We are too strong and powerful now, nothing can stop us. We expect plenty of trouble from the enemy, but we have too much on the ball for him to win. . . . We passed a big convoy today, it consisted of 116 ships. It was quite a sight. It means another big headache for the Japs. We got a big pan of cake from the bakers today. We had a party for ourselves, nothing is wasted out here, especially if it's sweet. Tennessee and Southern California play in the Rose Bowl today. The sea was very calm and the sunset was beautiful. What a sight.

January 4, 1945

They told us we will leave Leyte this afternoon for the invasion of Luzon[6]. . . . the biggest invasion in the Pacific so far. . . . General MacArthur is [with us] on the light cruiser Boise No. 47. . . . It must bring back memories as he sails along through the Philippines. It is over 3 years since he came through these same waters that we are passing through. The last time he came through here he received orders to leave Bataan and Corregidor on a PT boat for Australia.[7] Now his orders are to return and capture all the territory from the Japs. . . . This time he is riding on a big cruiser. . . .

January 9, 1945

It is very quiet, everyone is asleep. . . . We must be close to Lingayen Gulf.[8] Our troops did not sleep very good last night. This will be the last day on earth for a lot of them. They are so young and healthy now, and in a few hours many of them will be dead or wounded or crippled for life. Some will not even reach the beach. The Japs must have about 200,000 troops on Luzon. . . .

---

[6] Leyte and Luzon are islands in the Philippines. Luzon is the largest of the Philippine islands, and the location of Manila, the capital.

[7] MacArthur was ordered to leave the Philippines as Japanese forces gained control of the islands (See Document 28).

[8] This gulf on Luzon, northwest of Manila, was the site of an amphibious assault by American forces in January 1945, during which kamikaze attacks sank 24 ships and damaged 67.

February 21, 1945 *(Subic Bay)*[9]

The supply ship [that brought us food] had a group of various servicemen who were captured by the Japanese in 1942, and have been prisoners for all of these years. Many of them were wounded and all had white hair. They were nothing but "bags of bones." Their arms were like toothpicks. Some were very young, but looked much older than their years. All were very weak. . . .

August 8, 1945
(Off the coast of China)

All hands reported to stations at 1:30AM. . . . Jap planes were spotted in the immediate vicinity. . . . I almost forgot to mention that the greatest invention of the 20th century has been achieved. It's an atomic bomb. It was dropped on Hiroshima, Japan a couple of days ago, August 6. It wiped out everything for miles around. President Truman conveyed a warning to Japan to stop hostile actions but the Japanese refused. The Jap Premier ordered a special cabinet meeting right after the news of the bomb was relayed to him. The atomic bomb has the heat of the sun at its core. The pilots ten miles away could sense the concussion from it. Debris flew 40,000 feet into the air. Everyone is discussing the topic on board the Montpelier. The war may end soon now.[10]

August 10, 1945

We are still at Okinawa.[11] . . . At 8:50PM Captain Gorry spoke to the crew. He said that Japan would agree to our terms but wanted to keep the Emperor. They do not want anything to happen to him. When the Captain finished speaking, everyone gave a big cheer. Some of the men were whistling and yelling. There was plenty of rejoicing. Everyone went wild. Right after the men on Okinawa were informed of the news, we could hear guns firing, flares of all colors and star shells lit the sky. . . . They went wild over there. Some of the

---

[9] A bay on Luzon close to Manila, site of a large Naval base.
[10] See Document 31 for Truman's warning and Document 32 for his announcement of the atomic bomb.
[11] An island of Japan that is south of the main Japanese islands, Okinawa was the site of one of the bloodiest battles of the Pacific campaign. In 82 days of fighting, there were over 100,000 casualties, about 90 per cent of them Japanese.

ships here fired their guns and others blew their foghorns. It was quite a celebration. This was the happiest day of our lives. Everyone on the ship was having a great time. We did not have much sleep but we did not care.

October 22, 1945

During our two month stay in Japan, we visited many places and met many Japanese. The most famous place we visited was Hiroshima.[12] We were one of the first to see the extensive damage caused by the atomic bomb. . . . When we saw Hiroshima, a city of approximately half a million people, it was deserted except for a few people walking through with white cloths over their nose and mouths. I will never forget what I saw there. You have to see it. I cannot explain it. A few frames of buildings were the only thing that was left standing. Everything was ground to dust. . . . We passed a mother nursing her baby in the cellar of a destroyed house. She did not pay any attention to us as she sat there in the dust. Her whole family might have been wiped out and both of them might die later from the effects of the bomb. We felt very sorry for them. The only thing they owned was the clothes on their backs, and that was not much. We saw a few stumps of trees that were barren. They were completely black from burning. The trolley cars were blown off their tracks. Only they did not look like trolley cars anymore. They were completely destroyed. I could just see pieces of them. . . . Everything was reduced to a lot of rubble. . . . The enormous buildings with walls over a foot thick were all in small chunks. . . . As far as the eye could see there was nothing but destruction. The force from one of these bombs is fantastic. There is only one defense against the bomb, prevent it from falling. . . .

The Japanese people are honest, hard working people who were bluffed along by their cruel leaders. They were helpless to do anything about it. It was the Military Men. Their greed for power brought destruction down upon Japan. If they let the people run the government, it will be in good hands. The Japanese people are no different from the people in any other part of the world. The people all over the world are good. It's the leaders who are to blame. . . .

---

[12] Fahey returned home suffering from radiation poisoning as a result of his visit to Hiroshima.

Document 20

"Why Should We March?"
A. Philip Randolph
November 1942

A. Philip Randolph was a major figure in the labor movement, having founded the Brotherhood of Sleeping Car Porters, a union for African American train porters. Randolph believed in the use of collective non-violent action to improve the lot of the working class, including demonstrations and strikes. In this article, he proposed adopting a similar approach to combat racial discrimination. Randolph stressed the importance of using collective action to pressure the government to end racial discrimination while black soldiers and workers were needed to defend the nation. Randolph's essay appeared in the journal Survey Graphic *(1921–52), a progressive journal that published articles on various social issues.*

Source: A. Philip Randolph, "Why Should We March?" Survey Graphic 31 (November 1942), pp 488-89. https://goo.gl/ch5w2Q

The March on Washington Movement[1] has taken a leaf out of labor history in turning from industrial to political action. Its mass campaign is headed by the founder of the outstanding Negro union in the country: – *by the president of the Brotherhood of Sleeping Car Porters (AFL).*

Though I have found no Negroes who want to see the United Nations[2] lose this war, I have found many who, before the war ends, want to see the stuffing knocked out of white supremacy and of empire over subject peoples. American Negroes, involved as we are in the general issues of the conflict, are

---

[1] The name of the organization attempting to organize a march on Washington to protest segregation in the Armed Forces

[2] The term "United Nations" was first used in a statement issued January 1, 1942, by the United States, Great Britain, the USSR, and 23 other nations, pledging to continue fighting the Axis powers.

confronted not with a choice but with the challenge both to win democracy for ourselves at home and to help win the war for democracy the world over.

There is no escape from the horns of this dilemma. There ought not to be escape. For if the war for democracy is not won abroad, the fight for democracy cannot be won at home. If this war cannot be won for the white peoples, it will not be won for the darker races.

Conversely, if freedom and equality are not vouchsafed the peoples of color, the war for democracy will not be won. Unless this double-barreled thesis is accepted and applied, the darker races will never wholeheartedly fight for the victory of the United Nations. That is why those familiar with the thinking of the American Negro have sensed his lack of enthusiasm, whether among the educated or uneducated, rich or poor, professional or non-professional, religious or secular, rural or urban, north, south, east or west.

That is why questions are being raised by Negroes in church, labor union and fraternal society; in poolroom, barbershop, schoolroom, hospital, hairdressing parlor; on college campus, railroad, and bus. One can hear such questions asked as these: What have Negroes to fight for? What's the difference between Hitler and the "cracker" Talmadge of Georgia?[3] Why has a man got to be Jim Crowed to die for democracy? If you haven't got democracy yourself, how can you carry it to somebody else?

What are the reasons for this state of mind? The answer is: discrimination, segregation, Jim Crow. Witness the navy, the army, the air corps; and also government services at Washington. In many parts of the South, Negroes in Uncle Sam's uniform are being put upon, mobbed, sometimes even shot down by civilian and military people, and on occasion lynched. Vested political interests in race prejudice are so deeply entrenched that to them winning the war against Hitler is secondary to preventing Negroes from winning democracy for themselves. This is worth many divisions to Hitler and Hirohito.[4] While labor, business, and farm are subjected to ceilings and floors and not allowed to carry on as usual, these interests trade in the dangerous business of race and hate as usual.

When the defense program began and billions of taxpayers' money were appropriated for guns, ships, tanks, and bombs, Negroes presented themselves for work only to be given the cold shoulder. North as well as South, and despite qualifications, Negroes were denied skilled employment. Not until their wrath

---

[3] Eugene Talmadge (D) was the vehemently racist and anti-union governor of Georgia.

[4] Hirohito was the emperor of Japan.

and indignation took the form of a proposed protest march on Washington, scheduled for July 1, 1941, did things begin to move in the form of defense jobs for Negroes. The march was postponed by the timely issuance (June 25, 1941) of the famous Executive Order No. 8802 by President Roosevelt. But this order and the President's Committee on Fair Employment Practice, established thereunder, have as yet only scratched the surface by way of eliminating discriminations on account of race or color in war industry. Both management and labor unions in too many places and too many ways are still drawing the color line.

It is to meet this situation squarely with direct action that the March on Washington Movement launched its present program of protest mass meetings. Twenty thousand were in attendance at Madison Square Garden, June 16; sixteen thousand in the Coliseum in Chicago, June 26; nine thousand in the City Auditorium of St. Louis, August 14. Meetings of such magnitude were unprecedented among Negroes.[5] The vast throngs were drawn from all walks and levels of Negro life – businessmen, teachers, laundry workers, Pullman porters, waiters, and red caps[6]; preachers, crapshooters, and social workers; jitterbugs and Ph.D's. They came and sat in silence, thinking, applauding only when they considered the truth was told, when they felt strongly that something was going to be done about it.

The March on Washington Movement is essentially a movement of the people. It is all Negro and pro-Negro, but not for that reason anti-white or anti-Semitic, or anti-Catholic, or anti-foreign, or anti-labor. Its major weapon is the non-violent demonstration of Negro mass power. Negro leadership has united back of its drive for jobs and justice. "Whether Negroes should focus on Washington, and if so, when?" will be the focus of a forthcoming national conference. For the plan of a protest march has not been abandoned. Its purpose would be to demonstrate that American Negroes are in deadly earnest, and all out for their full rights. No power on earth can cause them today to abandon their fight to wipe out every vestige of second class citizenship and the dual standards that plague them.

A community is democratic only when the humblest and weakest person can enjoy the highest civil, economic, and social rights that the biggest and

---

[5] *Footnote in original:* In view of charges made that they were subsidized by Nazi funds, it may not be amiss to point out that of the $8,000 expenses of the Madison Square meeting every dime was contributed by Negroes themselves, except for tickets bought by some liberal white organizations.

[6] Railway station porters

most powerful possess. To trample on these rights of both Negroes and poor whites is such a commonplace in the South that it takes readily to anti-social, anti-labor, anti-Semitic and anti-Catholic propaganda. It was because of laxness in enforcing the Weimar constitution[7] in republican Germany that Nazism made headway. Oppression of the Negroes in the United States, like suppression of the Jews in Germany, may open the way for fascist dictatorship.

By fighting for their rights now, American Negroes are helping to make America a moral and spiritual arsenal for democracy. Their fight against the poll tax, against lynch law, segregation, and Jim Crow, their fight for economic, political, and social equality, thus becomes part of the global war for freedom.

PROGRAM OF THE MARCH ON WASHINGTON MOVEMENT

1. We demand, in the interest of national unity, the abrogation of every law which makes a distinction in treatment between citizens based on religion, creed, color, or national origin. This means an end to Jim Crow in education, in housing, in transportation and in every other social, economic, and political privilege; and especially, we demand, in the capital of the nation, an end to all segregation in public places and in public institutions.

2. We demand legislation to enforce the Fifth and Fourteenth Amendments guaranteeing that no person shall be deprived of life, liberty or property without due process of law, so that the full weight of the national government may be used for the protection of life and thereby may end the disgrace of lynching.

3. We demand the enforcement of the Fourteenth and Fifteenth Amendments and the enactment of the Pepper Poll Tax bill[8] so that all barriers in the exercise of the suffrage are eliminated.

4. We demand the abolition of segregation and discrimination in the army, navy, marine corps, air corps, and all other branches of national defense.

5. We demand an end to discrimination in jobs and job training. Further, we demand that the FEPC [Fair Employment Practices Committee][9] be made

---

[7] The Weimar Constitution was written and implemented in late 1918. Although it broadly extended the franchise, it granted "emergency" powers to the president that Hitler would exploit to gain autocratic power.

[8] Senator Claude Pepper (D-Florida) regularly introduced a bill to ban poll taxes in Federal elections. It regularly failed to gain support. In 1942, for example, his bill was filibustered by Southern Senators, and the Senate voted in November not to limit debate on it, effectively ending its chances of passage.

[9] See Document 21.

a permanent administrative agency of the U.S. Government and that it be given power to enforce its decisions based on its findings.

6. We demand that federal funds be withheld from any agency which practices discrimination in the use of such funds.

7. We demand colored and minority group representation on all administrative agencies so that these groups may have recognition of their democratic right to participate in formulating policies.

8. We demand representation for the colored and minority racial groups on all missions, political and technical, which will be sent to the peace conference so that the interests of all people everywhere may be fully recognized and justly provided for in the post-war settlement.

Document 21

Executive Order 9346 - Establishing a Committee on Fair Employment Practice
Franklin D. Roosevelt
May 27, 1943

The lack of a strong regulatory committee hampered efforts to combat racial discrimination in the defense industry. With the March on Washington Movement gaining momentum in late 1942 (Document 20), President Franklin D. Roosevelt issued Executive Order 9346 to replace the Fair Employment Practices Committee with the more powerful Committee on Fair Employment Practice. The old Committee had been part of the War Production Board and had limited authority. Executive Order 9346 established the Committee as a separate organization within the Office of the President, created regional offices around the United States, and gave the Committee jurisdiction over all Federal agencies.

Source: Franklin D. Roosevelt, "Executive Order 9346 Establishing a Committee on Fair Employment Practice," May 27, 1943. Online by Gerhard Peters and John T. Woolley, The American Presidency Project, https://goo.gl/fXakoo.

In order to establish a new Committee on Fair Employment Practice, to promote the fullest utilization of all available manpower, and to eliminate discriminatory employment practices, Executive Order No. 8802 of June 25, 1941, as amended by Executive Order No. 8823 of July 18, 1941, is hereby further amended to read as follows:

Whereas the successful prosecution of the war demands the maximum employment of all available workers regardless of race, creed, color, or national origin; and

Whereas it is the policy of the United States to encourage full participation in the war effort by all persons in the United States regardless of race, creed, color, or national origin, in the firm belief that the democratic way of life within the Nation can be defended successfully only with the help and support of all groups within its borders; and

Whereas there is evidence that available and needed workers have been barred from employment in industries engaged in war production solely by reason of their race, creed, color, or national origin, to the detriment of the prosecution of the war, the workers' morale, and national unity:

Now, Therefore, by virtue of the authority vested in me by the Constitution and statutes, and as President of the United States and Commander in Chief of the Army and Navy, I do hereby reaffirm the policy of the United States that there shall be no discrimination in the employment of any person in war industries or in Government by reason of race, creed, color, or national origin, and I do hereby declare that it is the duty of all employers, including the several Federal departments and agencies, and all labor organizations, in furtherance of this policy and of this Order, to eliminate discrimination in regard to hire, tenure, terms or conditions of employment, or union membership because of race, creed, color, or national origin.

It is hereby ordered as follows:

1. All contracting agencies of the Government of the United States shall include in all contracts hereafter negotiated or renegotiated by them a provision obligating the contractor not to discriminate against any employee or applicant for employment because of race, creed, color, or national origin and requiring him to include a similar provision in all subcontracts.

2. All departments and agencies of the Government of the United States concerned with vocational and training programs for war production shall take all measures appropriate to assure that such programs are administered without discrimination because of race, creed, color, or national origin.

3. There is hereby established in the Office for Emergency Management of the Executive Office of the President a Committee on Fair Employment Practice, hereinafter referred to as the Committee, which shall consist of a Chairman and not more than six other members to be appointed by the President. The Chairman shall receive such salary as shall be fixed by the President not exceeding $10,000 per year. The other members of the Committee shall receive necessary traveling expenses and, unless their compensation is otherwise prescribed by the President, a per diem allowance not exceeding $25 per day and subsistence expenses on such days as they are actually engaged in the performance of duties pursuant to this Order.

4. The committee shall formulate policies to achieve the purposes of this Order and shall make recommendations to the various Federal departments and agencies and to the President which it deems necessary and proper to make effective the provisions of this Order. The Committee shall also recommend to the Chairman of the War Manpower Commission appropriate

measures for bringing about the full utilization and training of manpower in and for war production without discrimination because of race, creed, color, or national origin.

5. The Committee shall receive and investigate complaints of discrimination forbidden by this Order. It may conduct hearings, make findings of fact, and take appropriate steps to obtain elimination of such discrimination.

6. Upon the appointment of the Committee and the designation of its Chairman, the Fair Employment Practice Committee established by Executive Order No. 8802 of June 25, 1941, hereinafter referred to as the old Committee, shall cease to exist. All records and property of the old Committee and such unexpended balances of allocations or other funds available for its use as the Director of the Bureau of the Budget shall determine shall be transferred to the Committee. The Committee shall assume jurisdiction over all complaints and matters pending before the old Committee and shall conduct such investigations and hearings as may be necessary in the performance of its duties under this Order.

7. Within the limits of the funds which may be made available for that purpose, the Chairman shall appoint and fix the compensation of such personnel and make provision for such supplies, facilities, and services as may be necessary to carry out this Order. The Committee may utilize the services and facilities of other Federal departments and agencies and such voluntary and uncompensated services as may from time to time be needed. The Committee may accept the services of State and local authorities and officials, and may perform the functions and duties and exercise the powers conferred upon it by this Order through such officials and agencies and in such manner as it may determine.

8. The Committee shall have the power to promulgate such rules and regulations as may be appropriate or necessary to carry out the provisions of this Order.

9. The provisions of any other pertinent Executive Order inconsistent with this Order are hereby superseded.

Document 22

Questions and Answers About the WAAC
United States Army Women's Auxiliary Corps
1943

The Women's Army Auxiliary Corps (WAACs) was created in 1942. Renamed the Women's Army Corps (WAC) shortly after this pamphlet was published by the War Department in 1943, the separate organization for women stayed in existence until 1978, when women were incorporated into previously all-male units. Approximately 150,000 women served in the WACs during World War II, but female officers could not command men. In 1943, recruiting into the WACs slowed due to widespread rumors that only disreputable women joined. This pamphlet was one attempt to change the image of WACs.

Source: United States Army Women's Auxiliary Corps, "73 Questions and Answers About the WAAC," World War II – Documents, Illinois State Library, item 11725223. https://goo.gl/2B64Tf

---

Here's everything you want to know about life in the WAAC. Here you'll find the answers to all your questions – about the work you'd do, the way you'd live, basic training, uniforms, pay, after-hours fun. Read every word! You'll see why joining the WAAC is so vitally important, why it can be the most exciting adventure of your life.

1. What Is the WAAC?

W-A-A-C stands for Women's Army Auxiliary Corps. When you join the WAAC, you work with the U. S. Army. No, not actually in the firing line. You don't pull any triggers or fire any cannons. But you take over Army tasks that are essential to help our fighting men win.

The organization of the WAAC is similar to Army organization. Your pay is the same as Army pay. You wear a uniform as snappy as any Army man's, and you're just as proud of it as he is!

Being a Waac is the biggest, most important job a girl can do in this war. To any girl with a true-blue heart, it's a challenge and the thrill of a lifetime!

2. Why Are Women Needed for Military Service?

It's true that in other wars the role of women has been a gentle one – to keep the home fires burning bright. But this war is different. It is more desperate and terrible than any war has ever been before. An urgent call has gone out from our Army. You, the women of America, are needed in the WAAC to serve with your soldiers. Can you fail to answer – when it may be within your power to help shorten the war and save the lives of American soldiers?

In the Army there are many vital tasks which you can do – tasks which can often be done better by women than by men. From Army officers everywhere come urgent messages: "The Waacs are doing a great job. Give us more." But there aren't enough Waacs to send. You are needed by our Army. You are needed now!

3. What Will I Do in the WAAC?

Any one of more than a hundred important jobs the men would have to do if you weren't there. Maybe you'll play nursemaid to a jeep and keep it in shipshape running order. Maybe your weather observations will be the "go ahead" for our bombers to take off. You may handle the coding of historic messages; drive Army officials on secret missions. Whatever you do, you'll know it's vital to winning the war!

. . . .

8. What Is Basic Training?

Basic training is your introduction to Army life. It gets you in good physical shape. Teaches you the "Emily Post"[1] of the Army. How to salute, and when. Military courtesy and Army customs. You'll have interesting study courses – about military operations and world events, about map reading, and safeguarding military information. You'll learn to talk a soldier's language on a lot of subjects – company administration, property responsibility, mess management, and many more. You'll learn about "close order drill" and special ceremonies. You'll work hard – plenty hard. And you'll love every minute of it! Every day, every hour you'll be learning something new.

9. Isn't Drilling Tough?

Your feet may protest a little, just for the first few days. But you won't. You'll love it. Every Waac does! You'll be amazed at how soon you learn to execute the orders . . . even though you never knew which foot was your left one before! And what a thrill you'll get when your company shows up best in Inspection Day parade!

---

[1] Emily Post (1872–1960) was a well-known etiquette expert.

. . . .

11. What Are the Specialist Schools?

At these schools you get more training to prepare you for one of the 142 specialist jobs that Waacs are doing. Perhaps you'll be sent to:

Administrative Specialist School. There you'll learn all the fascinating details of military procedure. How to handle secret information. How to keep important Army records. The Army way of taking letters.

Radio School is where you'll learn the intricacies of radio operation, code, and radio repairing. With training like this you'll be invaluable to the Army Air Forces or Signal Corps. And think what exciting careers there'll be in commercial radio when the war is over!

Bakers and Cooks School might make best use of your talents. There you learn to prepare quantity and quality meals. "Just like Mother used to make" – only much more of it. You'll get a real Army diploma when you finish the course. And if you want a job after the war, you'll have swell training for restaurant management, or for opening that tea room you've always dreamed of.

Motor Transport School might be for you. There'll be no mysteries left in an automobile by the time you're finished. You'll know all the inside workings of carburetors and transmissions. You'll learn all about driving, repairing and maintaining everything from a jeep to a 1½ ton truck. And when you get through, let any man dare to say, "Humph, a woman driver!" You'll match the best driver alive!

Army Music School is where WAAC band members (if they pass certain Army examinations) are trained to become WAAC band leaders. And how those girls can make "The Stars and Stripes Forever" boom!

Photo Lab Technicians School teaches you a variety of photographic skills – how to develop and print pictures, the techniques of making enlargements. After this course the Signal Corps will find you a mighty useful person. And you'll have training that ought to give you a fascinating career when the war is won.

12. Can I Become an Officer?

You bet you can, if you have the stuff. Officers are badly needed. Every girl who joins the WAAC has an equal chance to become one. You don't need a college degree. You don't even need a high school diploma – just the two years of high school or business school required for all members of the WAAC. At the end of your basic training, you can apply for Officer Candidate School if you've done well in basic training, and have been recommended by your Commanding Officer. Officers' training lasts six weeks.

Questions and Answers About the WAAC

. . . .

14. What Happens When I Go on Active Duty?

You may be assigned to an Army post, a famous airfield, an important Army headquarters office. You may serve in the United States or abroad.

You get a chance to say where you'd like to be stationed – overseas, within 300 miles of your home town, or anywhere in the United States. The WAAC will try to send you where you want to go, but the needs of the Service must naturally come first!

. . . .

22. Why Is WAAC Pay Better Than Average Civilian Pay?

Figure it out for yourself! Even as a WAAC auxiliary you get $50 a month – all clear! (And how often does a girl in civilian life have $50 left after the bills are paid?) Actually, that $50 is equal to about $35 a week in civilian life – since Waacs don't have to pay a penny for food, rent, or clothing.

As a Waac you never owe a bill to your dentist or your doctor. All medical services are free. If you need medicines or hospital care, Uncle Sam foots the bill!

23. What Extra Benefits Do I Get as a Waac?

You're entitled to government prices at the post exchange (that's the post department store). You get special rates at movies and theaters. "Furlough rates" on round trip railroad tickets – same as the Army. And from coast to coast you'll find hospitality waiting at the USO, Red Cross, and Service Clubs.

. . . .

31. May I Ever Wear Civilian Clothes?

Yes. In most places where Waacs are stationed, they're allowed to doff their uniforms when they're off duty and off the Post. But you'd be surprised how few of them want to! Once you see yourself in a WAAC uniform, you'll probably want to keep it on. Most Waacs are just plain proud of their uniforms ... and they get a real kick out of wearing them. Here's how one girl put it – "As a Waac, I feel like somebody."

. . . .

33. What Arrangements Are There for Going to Church?

At every WAAC Training Center and every Army post there are regular church services – Protestant, Catholic, and Jewish. You'll count your chaplain among your most valued friends.

34. With Whom May I Discuss Any Personal Problems?

Feel free to talk with your chaplain at any time. At WAAC Training Centers you can always go to see one of the Civilian Counselors who'll lend a motherly listening ear to any problem you want to talk over. All services of the American Red Cross are available to the WAAC – as to the Army.

35. May I Have Visitors?

Indeed you may – whenever you're off duty.

36. Are WAAC Regulations Stiff?

No, let's say they're sensible. You'll find most WAAC regulations are like Army Regulations – there's a common sense reason for every one of them. They're not just to cramp your style! And you'll probably discover there's a lot more freedom than you ever dreamed there would be! As a Waac, you're expected to be a responsible person – and you'll just naturally go out of your way to show people, "The Waacs are wonderful!"

37. May I Wear Jewelry?

Wedding ring, engagement ring or signet ring – yes! You may also wear a wrist watch, and an identification bracelet. No other jewelry, though. You wouldn't want any brighter glitter with your shining WAAC insignia.

38. Must My Hair Be Worn a Special Way?

Wear it any way that's natural and becoming. That's up to you. Just be sure it's neat and above your collar.

39. When Do I Wear My Hat?

Outdoors you wear your hat. Indoors you do as you'd do wearing civilian clothes – hat or no hat, either way.

40. May I Use Cosmetics?

Why not? The Army wants you to be attractive and feminine – not a dull, "washed-out Winnie." So go right ahead. Use your lipstick, your powder and rouge. Just use good taste and keep it inconspicuous. (Even in civilian life, you don't want to look like a painted doll.) Nail polish isn't frowned on either, as long as it's a lightish shade.

41. Is There Social Life in the WAAC? Will I Have Fun?

Bushels of it! The only trouble with a Waac's off-duty time, is that she usually has so many swell things to do, she can't tell which to choose. On an Army post, for instance, you'll go to Army dances, and probably get the rush of your life! You'll be invited to men's Service Club parties. You may be asked to visit Army classes, and share extra courses in such interesting things as radio code and camouflage. You'll get in on special entertainments staged by visiting movie and radio stars. You'll see the best movies – usually before they hit the big towns!

42. What About Extra Activities – Like Dramatics, Art and Music?

You'll find yourself with dozens of extra activities and hobby classes to choose from, if you want them. Glee Clubs. Classes in art, photography, languages, and leathercraft. And wait till you see the grand dramatic shows the Waacs take part in!

43. Are Dates With Army Men Allowed?

Of course. You'll have plenty! And with Navy men, Marines, and civilians, too! In Army camps, military custom prevails. WAAC auxiliaries and noncommissioned officers date enlisted men and noncoms. WAAC officers date Army officers.

44. What About Friends Who Are Officers?

If you're an auxiliary and have friends who are officers (either men or women) you can still be friends off duty. On duty, they're your superior officers, and you'll want to remember your "military manners," and act accordingly.

45. What Kind of Girls Will I Meet in the WAAC?

You'll meet all kinds of girls from all parts of the country. Girls who've traveled all over the world. Girls who've never been away from home before. You'll meet opera singers and secretaries. Milliners and movie actresses. Writers, teachers, artists, statisticians. The pick of America's girls are in the WAAC – you're bound to make friendships you'll value all your life.

46. Can a Married Woman Join the WAAC?

Indeed, yes – provided you have no dependents, no children under fourteen.

47. Can a Serviceman's Wife Join?

Of course! And she'll get a special thrill out of being in the WAAC – sharing her husband's experiences, and helping to get him home sooner! (And you can't blame her husband for being pretty proud of her!) Don't forget – servicemen's wives keep right on getting their monthly allotments while they're in the WAAC.

48. Can I Get Married While I'm in Service?

Of course you can. You can say "I do" at any time while you're in service. And the WAAC places no restrictions on whom you marry, either – Army man, Navy man, Marine, or civilian. That's your choice . . . .

. . . .

52. How Long Do I Serve?

The same as Army men. The WAAC term of service is for the duration of the war, plus six months afterwards.

. . . .

56. What Are the Requirements for Joining the WAAC?

Age: 21 to 44 years, inclusive.

Citizenship: You must be a citizen of the United States.

Marriage: You may be single or married.

Dependents: You must be without dependents; without children under 14.

Character: Must be excellent, of course.

Education: Two years of high school, business school, or similarly accredited school is required. (No high school or college diploma necessary.)

Health: Your health has to be good. You'll be given a physical examination at the Recruiting Center. Your height and weight should be average.

57. Why Should I Join the WAAC Right Away?

An imperative call has gone out from our Army. More Waacs are needed urgently – now! But there aren't enough to fill the demand. The faster you get in the WAAC, the more you can help to get the war won quickly and bring our soldiers home again. Looking at it selfishly – the faster you get in the WAAC the better your chances for quick promotion. (It's really an extra-special thrill to pin on those nice, shiny lieutenant's bars!)

58. Why Is the WAAC More Important Than Other War Work?

There are many jobs at home to be done in this war. Important jobs. Useful jobs. But there are many people who can do them. Older women, teenage girls, women ineligible for the WAAC.

Only a special group of women can serve in the WAAC. Only women without dependents – of a certain age and physical condition. If you fit the requirements, then joining the WAAC is the most important job you can do in this war. You, and only you, can help our soldiers where they need you most!

Document 23

"The Death of Captain Waskow"
Ernie Pyle
January 10, 1944

Journalist Ernie Pyle spent the war living among combat troops in North Africa, France, Italy, and the Pacific. Sharing their hardships and danger, he explained the war from their perspective. "The Death of Captain Waskow" captured the human cost of war and became one of his most popular newspaper columns. Pyle was killed coming ashore with troops during the Okinawa campaign on April 18, 1945, four months before the war ended.

Source: Ernie's War: The Best of Ernie Pyle's World War II Dispatches, edited by David Nichols (New York: Simon & Schuster, 1986), 195-97. Also *available from:* Reporting America at War, *television series by Insignia Film and WETA, Washington, DC, 2003. Reprinted with permission of the Scripps Howard Foundation.* https://goo.gl/HEk5Nf

---

AT THE FRONT LINES IN ITALY, January 10, 1944 – In this war I have known a lot of officers who were loved and respected by the soldiers under them. But never have I crossed the trail of any man as beloved as Capt. Henry T. Waskow of Belton, Texas.

Capt. Waskow was a company commander in the 36th Division. He had led his company since long before it left the States. He was very young, only in his middle twenties, but he carried in him a sincerity and gentleness that made people want to be guided by him.

"After my own father, he came next," a sergeant told me.

"He always looked after us," a soldier said. "He'd go to bat for us every time."

"I've never knowed him to do anything unfair," another one said.

I was at the foot of the mule trail the night they brought Capt. Waskow's body down. The moon was nearly full at the time, and you could see far up the trail, and even part way across the valley below. Soldiers made shadows in the moonlight as they walked.

Dead men had been coming down the mountain all evening, lashed onto the backs of mules. They came lying belly-down across the wooden pack-saddles, their heads hanging down on the left side of the mule, their stiffened legs sticking out awkwardly from the other side, bobbing up and down as the mule walked.

The Italian mule-skinners were afraid to walk beside dead men, so Americans had to lead the mules down that night. Even the Americans were reluctant to unlash and lift off the bodies at the bottom, so an officer had to do it himself, and ask others to help.

The first one came early in the morning. They slid him down from the mule and stood him on his feet for a moment, while they got a new grip. In the half light he might have been merely a sick man standing there, leaning on the others. Then they laid him on the ground in the shadow of the low stone wall alongside the road.

I don't know who that first one was. You feel small in the presence of dead men, and ashamed at being alive, and you don't ask silly questions.

We left him there beside the road, that first one, and we all went back into the cowshed and sat on water cans or lay on the straw, waiting for the next batch of mules.

Somebody said the dead soldier had been dead for four days, and then nobody said anything more about it. We talked soldier talk for an hour or more. The dead man lay all alone outside in the shadow of the low stone wall.

Then a soldier came into the cowshed and said there were some more bodies outside. We went out into the road. Four mules stood there, in the moonlight, in the road where the trail came down off the mountain. The soldiers who led them stood there waiting. "This one is Captain Waskow," one of them said quietly.

Two men unlashed his body from the mule and lifted it off and laid it in the shadow beside the low stone wall. Other men took the other bodies off. Finally there were five lying end to end in a long row, alongside the road. You don't cover up dead men in the combat zone. They just lie there in the shadows until somebody else comes after them.

The unburdened mules moved off to their olive orchard. The men in the road seemed reluctant to leave. They stood around, and gradually one by one I could sense them moving close to Capt. Waskow's body. Not so much to look, I think, as to say something in finality to him, and to themselves. I stood close by and I could hear.

One soldier came and looked down, and he said out loud, "God damn it." That's all he said, and then he walked away. Another one came. He said, "God damn it to hell anyway." He looked down for a few last moments, and then he turned and left.

Another man came; I think he was an officer. It was hard to tell officers from men in the half light, for all were bearded and grimy dirty. The man looked down into the dead captain's face, and then he spoke directly to him, as though he were alive. He said: "I'm sorry, old man."

Then a soldier came and stood beside the officer, and bent over, and he too spoke to his dead captain, not in a whisper but awfully tenderly, and he said:

"I sure am sorry, sir."

Then the first man squatted down, and he reached down and took the dead hand, and he sat there for a full five minutes, holding the dead hand in his own and looking intently into the dead face, and he never uttered a sound all the time he sat there.

And finally he put the hand down, and then reached up and gently straightened the points of the captain's shirt collar, and then he sort of rearranged the tattered edges of his uniform around the wound.

And then he got up and walked away down the road in the moonlight, all alone.

After that the rest of us went back into the cowshed, leaving the five dead men lying in a line, end to end, in the shadow of the low stone wall. We lay down on the straw in the cowshed, and pretty soon we were all asleep.

Document 24

Corporal Rupert Trimmingham's Letters to *Yank* Magazine

April 28, 1944 and July 28, 1944

Rupert Trimmingham's letters to Yank, a weekly magazine published by the U.S. military, laid bare the daily affronts that black soldiers encountered while serving their country in World War II. Nearly one million African Americans served in uniform during the war. The willingness of Yank, an offical publication, to publish his letter revealed the overall importance of black soldiers and workers to the war effort. Maintaining black morale required openly acknowledging that racial prejudice was a problem that existed. The double-victory campaign within the civil rights movement emphasized defeating facism abroad and racial discrimination at home.

Source: Rupert Trimmingham, letters to the editor, Yank, April 28, 1944 and July 28, 1944.

April 28, 1944
Dear *Yank*,

Here is a question that each Negro soldier is asking. What is the Negro soldier fighting for? On whose team are we playing? Myself and eight other soldiers were on our way from Camp Claiborne, La., to the hospital here at Fort Huachuca. We had to lay over until the next day for our train. On the next day we could not purchase a cup of coffee at any of the lunchrooms around there. As you know, Old Man Jim Crow rules. The only place where we could be served was at the lunchroom at the railroad station but, of course we had to go into the kitchen. But that's not all; 11:30 a.m. about a two dozen German prisoners of war, with two American guards, came into the station. They entered the lunchroom, sat at the tables, had their meals served, talked, smoked, in fact had quite a swell time. I stood on the outside looking on, and I could not help but ask myself these questions: Are these men sworn enemies of this country? Are they not taught to hate and destroy all democratic governments? Are we not American soldiers, sworn to fight for and die if need be for this country? Then why are they treated better than we are? Why are we pushed around like cattle? If we are fighting for the same thing, if we are to die for our country, then why does the Government allow such things to go on? Some of the boys are saying that you will not print this letter. I'm saying that you will.

Cpl. Rupert Trimmingham
Fort Huachuca, Ariz.

July 28, 1944
Dear *Yank*,

Allow me to thank you for publishing my letter. Although there was some doubt about its being published, yet somehow I felt that *Yank* was too great a paper not to. . . . Each day brings three, four or five letters to me in answer to my letter. I just returned from furlough and found 25 letters awaiting me. To date I've received 287 letters, and, strange as it may seem, 183 are from white men and women in the armed service. Another strange feature about these letters is that most of these people are from the Deep South. They are all proud of the fact that they are of the South but ashamed to learn that there are so many of their own people who by their actions and manner toward the Negro are playing Hitler's game. Nevertheless, it gives me new hope to realize that there are doubtless thousands of whites who are willing to fight this Frankenstein that so many white people are keeping alive. All that the Negro is asking for is to be given half a chance and he will soon demonstrate his worth to his country. Should these white people who realize that the Negro is a man who is loyal – one who would gladly give his life for this our wonderful country – would stand up, join with us and help us to prove to their white friends that we are worthy, I'm sure that we would bury race hate and unfair treatment. Thanks again.

Cpl. Rupert Trimmingham
Fort Huachuca, Ariz.

Document 25

D-Day Statement to the Allied Expeditionary Force
Dwight D. Eisenhower
June 5 - 6, 1944

On June 6, 1944 (known as D-Day) the Allied Forces launched a series of attacks on German-occupied northern France. A massive naval armada crossed the English Channel and troops stormed the beaches at Normandy from amphibious landing vehicles like the one shown in the photograph on page 84. Bad weather compounded the logistical difficulties of attacking the well-defended shoreline. Uncertain whether the attack would succeed, Allied Commander General Dwight D. Eisenhower prepared two messages on June 5, 1944. One was distributed to troops right after Eisenhower made the decision to attack at dawn. The second he scribbled in private to be released if the attack failed. The attacks secured a beachhead, so this second message was never issued.

Sources: Dwight D. Eisenhower, "D-day statement to soldiers, sailors, and airmen of the Allied Expeditionary Force, 6/44," Pre-Presidential Papers, 1916-1952, Dwight D. Eisenhower Library (Collection DDE-EPRE), National Archives and Records Administration. https://goo.gl/cF8gpY

Dwight D. Eisenhower, "In Case of Failure D-Day Message," Pre-Presidential Papers, Dwight D. Eisenhower Library (Principal File: Butcher Diary, 1942-1945; National Archives Identifier: 186470). https://goo.gl/chcbc2

Photo, "Into the Jaws of Death," Public Domain Photographs, 1882-1962, Franklin D. Roosevelt Library (National Archives Identifier: 195515). https://goo.gl/CxyFbC

D-Day Statement to the Allied Expeditionary Force

Order of the Day, June 6, 1944

"SUPREME HEADQUARTERS
ALLIED EXPEDITIONARY FORCE

Soldiers, Sailors, and Airmen of the Allied Expeditionary Force!

You are about to embark upon the Great Crusade, toward which we have striven these many months. The eyes of the world are upon you. The hope and prayers of liberty-loving people everywhere march with you. In company with our brave Allies and brothers-in-arms on other Fronts, you will bring about the destruction of the German war machine, the elimination of Nazi tyranny over the oppressed peoples of Europe, and security for ourselves in a free world.

Your task will not be an easy one. Your enemy is well trained, well equipped and battle-hardened. He will fight savagely.

But this is the year 1944! Much has happened since the Nazi triumphs of 1940-41. The United Nations[1] have inflicted upon the Germans great defeats, in open battle, man-to-man. Our air offensive has seriously reduced their strength in the air and their capacity to wage war on the ground. Our Home Fronts have given us an overwhelming superiority in weapons and munitions of war, and placed at our disposal great reserves of trained fighting men. The tide has turned! The free men of the world are marching together to Victory!

I have full confidence in your courage, devotion to duty and skill in battle. We will accept nothing less than full Victory!

Good luck! And let us beseech the blessing of Almighty God upon this great and noble undertaking.

Dwight D. Eisenhower

Hand-written, unissued message

Our landings in the Cherbourg-Havre area have failed to gain a satisfactory foothold and I have withdrawn the troops. My decision to attack at this time and place was based upon the best information available. The troops,

---

[1] The term "United Nations" was first used in a statement issued January 1, 1942, by the United States, Great Britain, the USSR, and 23 other nations, pledging to continue fighting the Axis powers.

the air and the Navy did all that bravery and devotion to duty could do. If any blame or fault attaches to the attempt it is mine alone.

Document 26

Stopping the Holocaust
August 9 and August 14, 1944

In January 1944, President Franklin D. Roosevelt created the War Refugee Board to aid civilian victims of Nazi aggression. The Board worked secretly with diplomats from neutral nations and resistance fighters to save the lives of approximately 200,000 Hungarian Jews. Jewish organizations, however, pressed the United States to do more. On August 9, 1944, the head of the Rescue Department of the World Jewish Congress, headquartered in New York, sent this note requesting that US airplanes drop bombs on Auschwitz-Birkenau, an extermination camp complex located in Poland. On August 14, 1944, the War Department rejected this request. The American Air Force soon thereafter bombed the I.G. Farben synthetic oil and rubber (Buna) works located only five miles from Auschwitz-Birkenau. The decision to not bomb Auschwitz continues to provoke debate over whether the United States did enough to help European Jews. One side emphasizes that air raids carried multiple risks including the likelihood of killing prisoners because American planes could not bomb with the pinpoint accuracy needed to hit only railroad lines. In addition, railway lines could be quickly rebuilt. The best way to end the killing was to win the war. Others argue that even if prisoners were killed, American bombing would have disrupted the Nazi killing machine and potentially saved the lives of those destined for the gas chambers.

Source: Letter from Assistant Secretary of War John McCloy to World Jewish Congress Rescue Department Head A. Leon Kubowitzki, World Jewish Congress Records, MS-361, Box D107, Folder 13, The Jacob Rader Marcus Center of the American Jewish Archives, Cincinnati, Ohio. Available online: https://goo.gl/gka9Nx

August 9, 1944
Hon. John J. McCloy
Under Secretary of War
War Department
Washington, D.C.

My dear Mr. Secretary:

I beg to submit to your consideration the following excerpt from a message which we received under date of July 29 from Mr. Ernest Frischer of the Czechoslovak State Council through the War Refugee Board.[1]

"I believe that destruction of gas chambers and crematoria in Oswiecim by bombing would have a certain effect now.[2] Germans are now exhuming and burning corpses in an effort to conceal their crimes. This could be prevented by destruction of crematoria and then Germans might possibly stop further mass exterminations especially since so little time is left to them. Bombing of railway communications in this same area would also be of importance and of military interest."

Sincerely yours,
A. Leon Kubowitzki
Head, Rescue Department

14 August 1944
Dear Mr. Kubowitski:

I refer to your letter of August 9 in which you request consideration of a proposal made by Mr. Ernest Frischer that certain installations and railroad centers be bombed.

The War Department had been approached by the War Refugee Board, which raised the question of the practicability of this suggestion. After a study it became apparent that such an operation could be executed only by the diversion of considerable air support essential to the success of our forces now

---

[1] The Czechoslovak State Council was a government in exile, set up in London after the German occupation of Czecholslovakia. Frischer, the only Jewish member of the council, had been chairman of the Jewish Party of Czechoslovakia from 1936 to 1939.

[2] Oswiecim is the Polish town where the Auschwitz-Birkenau death camp was located.

engaged in decisive operations elsewhere and would in any case be of such doubtful efficacy that it would not warrant the use of our resources. There has been considerable opinion to the effect that such an effort, even if practicable, might provoke even more vindictive action by the Germans.

The War Department fully appreciates the humanitarian motives which promoted the suggested operation, but for the reasons stated above it has not been felt that it can or should be undertaken, at least at this time.

Sincerely,
John J. McCloy
Assistant Secretary of War

Document 27

Manzanar: Excerpt from *Born Free and Equal*
Ansel Adams
1944

In 1943 the photographer Ansel Adams was granted limited access to Manzanar, a Japanese-American internment camp located in the foothills of the California Sierra-Nevada Mountains. He arrived just after a riot had rocked the camp and military authorities had administered a questionnaire to distinguish loyal from disloyal Japanese-Americans. Those inmates who answered questions incorrectly were deemed disloyal and shipped to another camp in Tule Lake. Japanese-Americans considered loyal were now allowed to leave the camp either by finding jobs, joining the military, or going to college.

To help re-assimilate Japanese-Americans into civilian life, Adams wanted to change public opinion so that communities would welcome rather than spurn these new arrivals. His photo essay, featuring 244 images with an accompanying narrative, had limited circulation during the war, however.

Source: Ansel Adams, Born Free and Equal: The Story of Loyal Japanese-Americans (NY: U.S. Camera, 1944), pp. 58-59; 63-67; 101. https://goo.gl/TNseGm

---

In any group of society the children are of greatest importance, and this importance is accentuated under abnormal conditions. The evacuation made family life difficult in many ways; it created for children of impressionable age environmental problems that will be hard to eradicate. However, from the start, education has been of major concern to the authorities and to the parents. At Manzanar the older evacuees built a tiny park with rabbits, chickens, and ducks, so little children would know a duck when they saw one. There is a "Children's Village" directed by Mr. Harry Haruto Matsumoto, where orphaned children from Alaska to San Diego find a home. Evacuation struck the very young and the very old. Newborn babies as well as the oldest persons were moved with all others. Kindergartens, grammar schools and high schools were established under the direction of Doctor Genevieve Carter of the Manzanar Educational Division. Hence there has been little interruption in the normal school life of the children, and the usual extra-curricular activities have not been neglected. The Manzanar High School is accredited to the University of California, even though its graduates are barred from that university by military restrictions. Plays, concerts, the Manzanar High School Choir under the able direction of Louis Frizzell, and a wide list of sports, keep the young people occupied and interested. The older residents play or are spectators at judo, kendo, tennis, basketball, football, and the universal enthusiasm – baseball. There is a golf links, unique in that there is no grass – only the desert earth. The greens are built up of sifted soil, and it all seems to work out satisfactorily, although there are certain difficult decisions to be made as to what constitutes "fairway" or "rough." A new auditorium has been completed recently and movies, music, and drama are accented in the recreation program. There are no class or age distinctions at Manzanar, and toddlers will be seen sitting next to benign old gentlemen at an outdoor band concert, or thronging with their elders into an exhibit at the Visual Education Museum. Only those employed on the farms may pass beyond the confines of the Residential section, hence the emphasis on organized sport rather than on excursions and walking tours. Victory gardens and the Pleasure Park are the concern of groups who are able to work at them; the latter is an ambitious undertaking – pools, greenery, walks and a pavilion created in the barren soil of the desert within the confines of the Center. Under special permit trees and stones were brought many miles from the Sierra and set about with that persuasive informal formality of the traditional Japanese garden.

Another person associated with the Manzanar Hospital whom I would like to bring to your attention is Michael Koichi Yonemitsu, X-ray technician. Born in Los Angeles in 1915, he majored for three years in engineering, and hopes eventually to complete his studies and specialize in X-ray. Coming from an intelligent and well-to-do gamily and enjoying a secure life with an apparently clear and well-planned future before him, Michael Yonemitsu found the evacuation difficult to reconcile with his concept of American life. However, he has adjusted himself admirably to conditions beyond his control. He would like to see the future evidence a "return to sound economic levels, fair trade, and subsequent raising of world living standards; . . . a better understanding between all people to ease racial prejudice; and a move toward greater religious tolerances." Speaking of the Japanese-American Combat Team he says, "My brother is in that combat team, I figure this is a chance to show his loyalty."

Visiting Michael's home, we shall meet his father and sister. This home is perhaps fitted out a bit better than the average; there is a fine radio-phonograph, a good collection of classical recordings, and some simple modern chairs and bookcases. Through their sunny window they look out on orchards and the North Farm. Mr. Francis Yonemitsu, father of Michael, was born in Japan. He is not and cannot be a citizen. But he is American in spirit, and he is a realist. In regard to his pre-war life in America he said he would have liked to be truly assimilated, but that the Caucasians themselves prevented it. He was automatically barred from many public places. As to the future he says, "At present I am undecided. I leave my children's plans up to them. They are citizens; my problem is far more difficult." Mr. Yonemitsu hopes that in the post-war world "our federal government will take steps to smooth out once and for all the minority problems of the Japanese, Negroes, etc. . . . Religion is valuable and we should attempt to further religion. Faith should be the guiding factor in our lives." (The Yonemitsu family is Catholic.)

On top of their phonograph I found a picture of Our Saviour, a photograph of Robert Yonemitsu in the uniform of an American soldier, and some of his letters to his sister Lucy. I photographed them just as they were. The picture tells much about the Yonemitsu family, and about many other such families as well. Father Yonemitsu says about the combat team: "My son Robert is in the combat team. I am hoping he will be a credit to me and to the Japanese-American people. I hope he will help to show that the Americans of Japanese ancestry are as loyal as any other Americans."

Conclusion

Perhaps we find it difficult to visualize the life and mental attitudes of the evacuees. We are, in the main, protected and established in security considerably above other peoples. We take Americanism for granted; only when civil duties such as military service, jury duty, or the irksome payment of taxes, confront us do we sense the existence of government and authority. We go through conventional gestures of patriotism, discuss the Constitution with casual conviction, contradict our principles with the distortions of race prejudices and class distinctions, and otherwise escape the implications of our civilization. America will take care of us, America is as stable as the mountains, as severely eternal as the ocean and the sky! In times of war we sacrifice magnificently; in times of peace we prey upon one another with sincerity and determination. The world has seldom seen our superior in intellect and accomplishment, nor has it seen our inferior in many aspects of human relationships. Only when our foundations are shaken, our lives distorted by some great catastrophe, do we become aware of the potentials of our system and our government.

Document 28

Radio Address Upon Returning to the Philippines
General Douglas MacArthur
October 20, 1944

In March 1942, with the Japanese on the verge of conquering the Philippines (then an American colony), President Franklin D. Roosevelt ordered General Douglas MacArthur, Commander of American Army Forces in the Far East, to leave Corregidor island in Manila Bay, to which he had withdrawn as the Japanese advanced. Upon his arrival in Australia, MacArthur vowed, "I shall return." On October 20, 1944, MacArthur waded ashore in the Leyte Gulf as American troops landed to re-take the Philippines. He immediately delivered this radio address.

Source: AmericanVoices, Vincent Voice Library, MATRIX: The Center for Humane Arts, Letters and Social Sciences, Michigan State University https://goo.gl/LaAt4q

TO THE PEOPLE OF THE PHILIPPINES:

I have returned. By the grace of Almighty God our forces stand again on Philippine soil – soil consecrated in the blood of our two peoples. We have come, dedicated and committed, to the task of destroying every vestige of enemy control over your daily lives, and of restoring, upon a foundation of indestructible strength, the liberties of your people.

At my side is your President, Sergio Osmena, worthy successor of that great patriot, Manuel Quezon, with members of his cabinet.[1] The seat of your government is now therefore firmly re-established on Philippine soil.

The hour of your redemption is here. Your patriots have demonstrated an unswerving and resolute devotion to the principles of freedom that challenges the best that is written on the pages of human history. I now call upon your supreme effort that the enemy may know from the temper of an aroused and

---

[1] Manuel Quezon was president of the Philippines when the Japanese invaded and headed the Filipino government-in-exile until he died in April 1944 of tuberculosis.

outraged people within that he has a force there to contend with no less violent than is the force committed from without.

Rally to me. Let the indomitable spirit of Bataan and Corregidor lead on.[2] As the lines of battle roll forward to bring you within the zone of operations, rise and strike. Strike at every favorable opportunity. For your homes and hearths, strike! For future generations of your sons and daughters, strike! In the name of your sacred dead, strike! Let no heart be faint. Let every arm be steeled. The guidance of divine God points the way. Follow in His Name to the Holy Grail of righteous victory!

Douglas MacArthur

---

[2] After long resistance, the surrender of American and Filipino troops in Bataan (April 1942) and Corregidor (May 1942) had completed the Japanese conquest.

Document 29

Korematsu v. US
December 18, 1944

Toyosaburo Korematsu challenged his conviction for defying an evacuation order in 1942, and his case made it up to the Supreme Court. In the majority decision, the Supreme Court avoided ruling on whether the overall internment of Japanese-Americans was constitutional. The majority decision focused solely on whether Korematsu could legally refuse to report to an assembly center. The dissenting opinions, however, declared internment unconstitutional and racially-based. On the same day, the Court ruled in the case of Mitsye Endo that the government could not detain loyal citizens. A day before the rulings, President Franklin D. Roosevelt rescinded Executive Order 9066 (Document 16), which had authorized both the removal and internment of the Japanese.

Source: 323 U.S. 214 (1944). Legal Information Institute, Cornell Law School. https://goo.gl/eMj7eS

Mr. Justice Black[1] delivered the opinion of the Court.

The petitioner, an American citizen of Japanese descent, was convicted in a federal district court for remaining in San Leandro, California, a "Military Area," contrary to Civilian Exclusion Order No. 34 of the Commanding General of the Western Command, U.S. Army, which directed that after May 9, 1942, all persons of Japanese ancestry should be excluded from that area. No question was raised as to petitioner's loyalty to the United States. The Circuit Court of Appeals affirmed and the importance of the constitutional question involved caused us to grant certiorari.[2]

It should be noted, to begin with, that all legal restrictions which curtail the civil rights of a single racial group are immediately suspect. That is not to

---

[1] Hugo Black (1886–1971) served as a Supreme Court Justice from 1937 to 1971.
[2] "Certiorari" literally means "to be shown." When the Supreme Court "grants certiorari," it asks the lower court to send it all documents relevant to a case so that it can review them. In effect, it signals that it will hear an appeal. The Supreme Court chooses to hear only those cases that at least three justices feel present a federal question of public interest.

say that all such restrictions are unconstitutional. It is to say that courts must subject them to the most rigid scrutiny. Pressing public necessity may sometimes justify the existence of such restrictions; racial antagonism never can.

In the instant case prosecution of the petitioner was begun by information charging violation of an Act of Congress, of March 21, 1942, 56 Stat. 173, 18 U.S.C.A. 97a, which provides that "... whoever shall enter, remain in, leave, or commit any act in any military area or military zone prescribed, under the authority of an Executive Order of the President, by the Secretary of War, or by any military commander designated by the Secretary of War, contrary to the restrictions applicable to any such area or zone or contrary to the order of the Secretary of War or any such military commander, shall, if it appears that he knew or should have known of the existence and extent of the restrictions or order and that his act was in violation thereof, be guilty of a misdemeanor and upon conviction shall be liable to a fine of not to exceed $5,000 or to imprisonment for not more than one year, or both, for each offense."

... In *Kiyoshi Hirabayashi v. United States*,[3] ... we sustained a conviction obtained for violation of the curfew order. The Hirabayashi conviction and this one thus rest on the same 1942 Congressional Act and the same basic executive and military orders, all of which orders were aimed at the twin dangers of espionage and sabotage.

The 1942 Act was attacked in the Hirabayashi case as an unconstitutional delegation of power; it was contended that the curfew order and other orders on which it rested were beyond the war powers of the Congress, the military authorities and of the President, as Commander in Chief of the Army; and finally that to apply the curfew order against none but citizens of Japanese ancestry amounted to a constitutionally prohibited discrimination solely on account of race. To these questions, we gave the serious consideration which their importance justified. We upheld the curfew order as an exercise of the power of the government to take steps necessary to prevent espionage and sabotage in an area threatened by Japanese attack.

In the light of the principles we announced in the Hirabayashi case, we are unable to conclude that it was beyond the war power of Congress and the Executive to exclude those of Japanese ancestry from the West Coast war area at the time they did. True, exclusion from the area in which one's home is located is a far greater deprivation than constant confinement to the home

---

[3] In *Kiyoshi Hirabayashi v. United States* (1943), the Supreme Court upheld the constitutionality of curfew laws aimed at specific groups during times of war.

from 8 p.m. to 6 a.m. Nothing short of apprehension by the proper military authorities of the gravest imminent danger to the public safety can constitutionally justify either. But exclusion from a threatened area, no less than curfew, has a definite and close relationship to the prevention of espionage and sabotage. The military authorities, charged with the primary responsibility of defending our shores, concluded that curfew provided inadequate protection and ordered exclusion. They did so, as pointed out in our Hirabayashi opinion, in accordance with Congressional authority to the military to say who should, and who should not, remain in the threatened areas....

Like curfew, exclusion of those of Japanese origin was deemed necessary because of the presence of an unascertained number of disloyal members of the group, most of whom we have no doubt were loyal to this country. It was because we could not reject the finding of the military authorities that it was impossible to bring about an immediate segregation of the disloyal from the loyal that we sustained the validity of the curfew order as applying to the whole group. In the instant case, temporary exclusion of the entire group was rested by the military on the same ground....

... [H]ardships are part of war, and war is an aggregation of hardships. All citizens alike, both in and out of uniform, feel the impact of war in greater or lesser measure. Citizenship has its responsibilities as well as its privileges, and in time of war the burden is always heavier. Compulsory exclusion of large groups of citizens from their homes, except under circumstances of direst emergency and peril, is inconsistent with our basic governmental institutions. But when under conditions of modern warfare our shores are threatened by hostile forces, the power to protect must be commensurate with the threatened danger.

... It is now argued that the validity of the exclusion order cannot be considered apart from the orders requiring [Korematsu], after departure from the area, to report and to remain in an assembly or relocation center. The contention is that we must treat these separate orders as one and inseparable; that, for this reason, if detention in the assembly or relocation center would have illegally deprived the petitioner of his liberty, the exclusion order and his conviction under it cannot stand.

We are thus being asked to pass at this time upon the whole subsequent detention program in both assembly and relocation centers, although the only issues framed at the trial related to petitioner's remaining in the prohibited area in violation of the exclusion order. Had petitioner here left the prohibited area and gone to an assembly center we cannot say either as a matter of fact or law, that his presence in that center would have resulted in his detention in a relocation center. Some who did report to the assembly center were not sent to relocation centers but were released upon condition that they remain outside the prohibited zone until the military orders were modified or lifted. This illustrates that they pose different problems and may be governed by different principles. The lawfulness of one does not necessarily determine the lawfulness of the others. ...

It is said that we are dealing here with the case of imprisonment of a citizen in a concentration camp solely because of his ancestry, without evidence or inquiry concerning his loyalty and good disposition towards the United States. Our task would be simple, our duty clear, were this a case involving the imprisonment of a loyal citizen in a concentration camp because of racial prejudice. Regardless of the true nature of the assembly and relocation centers – and we deem it unjustifiable to call them concentration camps with all the ugly connotations that term implies – we are dealing specifically with nothing but an exclusion order. To cast this case into outlines of racial prejudice, without reference to the real military dangers which were presented, merely confuses the issue. Korematsu was not excluded from the Military Area because of hostility to him or his race. He was excluded because we are at war with the Japanese Empire, because the properly constituted military authorities feared an invasion of our West Coast and felt constrained to take proper security measures, because they decided that the military urgency of the situation demanded that all citizens of Japanese ancestry be segregated from the West Coast temporarily, and finally, because Congress, reposing its confidence in this time of war in our military leaders – as inevitably it must – determined that they should have the power to do just this. There was evidence of disloyalty on the part of some, the military authorities considered that the need for action was great, and time was short. We cannot – by availing ourselves of the calm perspective of hindsight – now say that at that time these actions were unjustified.

AFFIRMED

Mr. Justice Roberts.[4]

I dissent, because I think the indisputable facts exhibit a clear violation of Constitutional rights.

This is not a case of keeping people off the streets at night as was *Kiyoshi Hirabayashi v. United States*. . . . On the contrary, it is the case of convicting a citizen as a punishment for not submitting to imprisonment in a concentration camp, based on his ancestry, and solely because of his ancestry, without evidence or inquiry concerning his loyalty and good disposition towards the United States. If this be a correct statement of the facts disclosed by this record, and facts of which we take judicial notice, I need hardly labor the conclusion that Constitutional rights have been violated.

The Government's argument, and the opinion of the court, in my judgment, erroneously divide that which is single and indivisible and thus make the case appear as if the petitioner violated a Military Order, sanctioned by Act of Congress, which excluded him from his home, by refusing voluntarily to leave and, so, knowingly and intentionally, defying the order and the Act of Congress.

The petitioner, a resident of San Leandro, Alameda County, California, is a native of the United States of Japanese ancestry who, according to the uncontradicted evidence, is a loyal citizen of the nation. . . .

[On] March 27, 1942, by Proclamation No. 4, the General[5] recited that "it is necessary, in order to provide for the welfare and to insure the orderly evacuation and resettlement of Japanese voluntarily migrating from Military Area No. 1 to restrict and regulate such migration"; and ordered that, as of March 29, 1942, "all alien Japanese and persons of Japanese ancestry who are within the limits of Military Area No. 1, be and they are hereby prohibited from leaving that area for any purpose until and to the extent that a future proclamation or order of this headquarters shall so permit or direct."

No order had been made excluding the petitioner from the area in which he lived. By Proclamation No. 4 he was, after March 29, 1942, confined to the limits of Area No. 1. If the Executive Order No. 9066 and the Act of Congress meant what they said, to leave that area, in the face of Proclamation No. 4, would be to commit a misdemeanor.

May 3, 1942, General DeWitt issued Civilian Exclusion Order No. 346 providing that, after 12 o'clock May 8, 1942, all persons of Japanese ancestry,

---

[4] Owen Roberts (1875–1955) served as a Supreme Court Justice from 1930 to 1945.
[5] General John L. Dewitt, Commander of the Western Defense Command, who issued the orders for removal and detention of Americans of Japanese ancestry.

both alien[6] and non-alien, were to be excluded from a described portion of Military Area No. 1. . . . The obvious purpose of the orders made, taken together, was to drive all citizens of Japanese ancestry into Assembly Centers within the zones of their residence, under pain of criminal prosecution. The predicament in which the petitioner thus found himself was this: He was forbidden, by Military Order, to leave the zone in which he lived; he was forbidden, by Military Order, after a date fixed, to be found within that zone unless he were in an Assembly Center located in that zone. General DeWitt's report to the Secretary of War concerning the program of evacuation and relocation of Japanese makes it entirely clear, if it were necessary to refer to that document, – and, in the light of the above recitation, I think it is not, – that an Assembly Center was a euphemism for a prison. No person within such a center was permitted to leave except by Military Order.

In the dilemma that he dare not remain in his home, or voluntarily leave the area, without incurring criminal penalties, and that the only way he could avoid punishment was to go to an Assembly Center and submit himself to military imprisonment, the petitioner did nothing. . . .

As I have said above, the petitioner, prior to his arrest, was faced with two diametrically contradictory orders given sanction by the Act of Congress of March 21, 1942. The earlier of those orders made him a criminal if he left the zone in which he resided; the later made him a criminal if he did not leave.

I had supposed that if a citizen was constrained by two laws, or two orders having the force of law, and obedience to one would violate the other, to punish him for violation of either would deny him due process of law. And I had supposed that under these circumstances a conviction for violating one of the orders could not stand. . . .

I would reverse the judgment of conviction.

Mr. Justice MURPHY,[7] dissenting.

This exclusion of "all persons of Japanese ancestry, both alien and non-alien," from the Pacific Coast area on a plea of military necessity in the absence of martial law ought not to be approved. Such exclusion goes over "the very brink of constitutional power" and falls into the ugly abyss of racism. . . .

It must be conceded that the military and naval situation in the spring of 1942 was such as to generate a very real fear of invasion of the Pacific Coast,

---

[6] An alien is anyone not a citizen of the United States.
[7] William Murphy (1890–1949) served as a Supreme Court Justice from 1940 to 1949.

Korematsu v. US

accompanied by fears of sabotage and espionage in that area. The military command was therefore justified in adopting all reasonable means necessary to combat these dangers. In adjudging the military action taken in light of the then apparent dangers, we must not erect too high or too meticulous standards; it is necessary only that the action have some reasonable relation to the removal of the dangers of invasion, sabotage and espionage. But the exclusion, either temporarily or permanently, of all persons with Japanese blood in their veins has no such reasonable relation. And that relation is lacking because the exclusion order necessarily must rely for its reasonableness upon the assumption that all persons of Japanese ancestry may have a dangerous tendency to commit sabotage and espionage and to aid our Japanese enemy in other ways. It is difficult to believe that reason, logic or experience could be marshalled in support of such an assumption....

The military necessity which is essential to the validity of the evacuation order thus resolves itself into a few intimations that certain individuals actively aided the enemy, from which it is inferred that the entire group of Japanese Americans could not be trusted to be or remain loyal to the United States. No one denies, of course, that there were some disloyal persons of Japanese descent on the Pacific Coast who did all in their power to aid their ancestral land. Similar disloyal activities have been engaged in by many persons of German, Italian and even more pioneer stock in our country. But to infer that examples of individual disloyalty prove group disloyalty and justify discriminatory action against the entire group is to deny that under our system of law individual guilt is the sole basis for deprivation of rights. Moreover, this inference, which is at the very heart of the evacuation orders, has been used in support of the abhorrent and despicable treatment of minority groups by the dictatorial tyrannies which this nation is now pledged to destroy. To give constitutional sanction to that inference in this case, however well-intentioned may have been the military command on the Pacific Coast, is to adopt one of the cruelest of the rationales used by our enemies to destroy the dignity of the individual and to encourage and open the door to discriminatory actions against other minority groups in the passions of tomorrow. No adequate reason is given for the failure to treat these Japanese Americans on an individual basis by holding investigations and hearings to separate the loyal from the disloyal, as was done in the case of persons of German and Italian ancestry. See House Report No. 2124 (77th Cong., 2d Sess.) 247-52. It is asserted merely that the loyalties of this group "were unknown and time was of the essence." Yet nearly four months elapsed after Pearl Harbor before the first exclusion order was issued; nearly eight months went by until the last order was issued; and the last of these "subversive" persons was not actually removed until almost eleven months had elapsed. Leisure and deliberation seem to have been more of the essence than speed. And the fact that conditions were not such as to warrant a declaration of martial law adds strength to the belief that the factors of time and military necessity were not as urgent as they have been represented to be....

I dissent, therefore, from this legalization of racism. Racial discrimination in any form and in any degree has no justifiable part whatever in our democratic way of life. It is unattractive in any setting but it is utterly revolting among a free people who have embraced the principles set forth in the Constitution of the United States. All residents of this nation are kin in some way by blood or culture to a foreign land. Yet they are primarily and necessarily a part of the new and distinct civilization of the United States. They must accordingly be treated at all times as the heirs of the American experiment and as entitled to all the rights and freedoms guaranteed by the Constitution.

Document 30

"Do You Want Your Wife to Work After the War?"
G. I. Roundtable Series
1944

Army morale program officers organized debates over pressing issues of the day as part of off-duty education programs that gave soldiers opportunities to use their free time productively. These G.I. roundtables also reminded soldiers that one day they would return home to their civilian lives. This pamphlet offered guidance for holding a debate on the question, "Do you want your wife to work after the war?" This debate reflected the reality that 19 million women were in the workforce during the war, while 16 million men served in the armed forces. Most of these female workers had shifted jobs during the war, moving into better paying and more highly skilled positions formerly held by men.

Source: "Do You Want Your Wife to Work After the War?" G. I. Roundtable Series, EM31, War Department Education Manual, 1944, p. 17–28; 22–31. Available from Illinois Digital Archives, https://goo.gl/jLdaVH

WARTIME WIVES

The war has drawn vast armies of women from their homes into jobs of all sorts. The number of working women has increased 25 per cent during the past three years. Today women hold one in every three civilian jobs in the country. War has given them new motives, stirred up new problems, brought about new adjustments.

"There are two things I want to be sure of after the war," writes a soldier from the South Pacific. "I want my wife waiting for me and I want my job waiting for me. I don't want to find my wife busy with a job that some returning soldier needs, and I don't want to find that some other man's wife has my job."

What will men like this one actually find when they come home? Will their wives be only too glad to give up their strenuous jobs in war plants to return to the job of being homemakers? Or will they continue to work outside the home? If they must or prefer to stay at home again what will be done to make the tasks of homemaking more attractive? If a woman wants to keep on working after the war what will her husband's attitude be? If there are no longer jobs enough for everyone should a married woman be allowed to work? Does she have as much right as her husband to try to find the work she wants? These are only a few of the questions that must be faced when the war is over ....

TRIAL BY DEBATE

In a democracy, controversial issues are not decided by decrees of dictators or even by cold facts arrayed in formidable statistical tables. Democracy in one sense is government by discussion and it is through the disputes of men on the street and in the service that ultimate decisions are shaped. It is the thoughts and the feelings of the everyday men and women that count in the long run. Let's listen in on a squabble in an American camp, behind the lines in Italy, or perhaps on an American transport. Says Pvt. Pro, glancing up from an ancient American newspaper, "Say, you know with the way prices are going up I'm going to have to send my wife out to work after the war. I may not be able to buy myself a good suit of civies to say nothing of one of those helicopters unless the wife brings home a little bacon on Saturday night."

Pvt. Con glares at Pvt. Pro, "Look here, Pro, where I come from we don't send our wives out to work. If I can't make enough money to support a wife, I just don't expect to be married. My mother had plenty to do right around the house, and she didn't take in washing either. Maybe you're just too lazy to go and dig out a decent income. I'm not like that. I'm for the good old-fashioned way. I'll pay for the food and the wife can cook it, and what is more, cook it the way I like it. A lot of these women who have been out trying to do a man's job are going to be glad to go back home and be supported by some good man."

Pvt. Pro disagrees, "All right, Con, you wait and see how long it takes to save up enough money to get married on in the way you look at it. You're not going to get any bonus that will buy a bungalow for the little woman. Furniture costs money. Of course, every girl expects to have a car. Your lady friend has probably been making big dough in a war plant and has gotten used to having a new hat once in a while. 'When the nylons bloom again,' she is going to want a few pairs. If you wait to do everything right, you'll probably find that the girl won't. Besides you'll be too old to mow your own lawn by the time you save up enough for a house. If the girl likes to work, why stop her? You can get married sooner if there are two people to face the bill collector. A woman appreciates things a lot more if she has had something to do with paying for them. You know it's not the Civil War but World War II that you are in. It just isn't going to be the same kind of world when this thing is over."

Pvt. Con protests, "So you think you've got it all figured out. How about competition from these women that are staying on the job to support guys like you? They're going to make it harder for me to do it my way. Maybe your wife does help out, but if enough women are out gunning for jobs you'll get such a measly pay check that you're right back where you were before. That's the way it was during the depression – a man couldn't get a job and if he did he couldn't make enough money to support a family; there was always a woman who could afford to work just a bit cheaper. A fellow went to jail if he didn't support his family and he couldn't support them because some other fellow's wife was working in an office to earn herself a fur coat."

Pvt. Pro is disgusted. "If most men thought the cockeyed way you do," he says, "you'd expect women to get the jobs. Plenty of women can think straighter than you do. Why do you suppose a lot of women go to work during a war? To make everybody poorer? The more people you've got at work the more things get produced. If a wife works she's got money to spend which creates some more jobs. She can hire a maid. She can buy an automobile and even a dumb cluck like you may get a job putting it together."

From Pvt. Con, "All right, Pro, but don't forget that automobiles aren't the only things that need to be produced. How about kids? If women don't have kids, pretty soon there won't be any automobiles nor anybody to ride in them. A woman just can't do everything. We need a lot of babies to make up for this war. Sure, you hear a lot about women who have become big shots. They make the headlines, hold big jobs, write books, perhaps become scientists, but do they have children? I bet they don't pass on their brains to very many youngsters."

Pvt. Pro objects, "Well, why expect all women to do the same thing? You don't expect all men to run locomotives or all of them to work on a farm. Women have got all kinds of different abilities. A lot of them have been going to school, while you and I were out here. Why waste a college education on a floor mop? If a woman can run a store or teach school, she can have kids just the same, because she's got money to hire somebody to help out at home who likes that sort of thing and can't do anything else."

Pvt. Con breaks in, "That's just where you are wrong. You can't hire anybody to do a really bang-up job of making a home and bringing kids up right. If the mother isn't on the job, the children may get into trouble, get hurt, eat the wrong things. A man doesn't have much of a home either when his wife is out on the job. His buttons don't get sewed on and if he wants to step out and have a little fun in the evening the wife is just too tired or interested in something else. A man wants a wife, not a business partner."

Pvt. Pro retorts, "How would you like to stay at home all day, keep the kids out of mischief, and wash the same old dishes day after day? A woman is more interesting if she has a job too. There is a little variety; she knows what is going on in the world. With her own pay check she can do things and buy things without asking her husband's permission or picking his pockets to get the price of a movie."

Pvt. Con disagrees, "Pro, you just can't seem to get it through your head that there are two kinds of jobs in the world and two kinds of people for these jobs. One job is to get into the outside world, make a living, know what's going on. The other job is to keep the home fires burning, to make a house into a home, to make children feel that they belong there, and to give a husband something worth coming home to. A real woman who isn't spoiled by newfangled ideas just naturally wants children and likes to mother them. The job has to be done and women are best fitted for the job."

Remarks Pro, "I catch on, Con. You're just on the wrong side of this war. You and Hitler are buddies. He had a revelation, too, about what women should be like.[1] According to the kind of democracy I was taught to believe in, American citizens have a right to choose their opportunities and to make the most of them even if they are women."

"Look, Pro, you've got me all wrong. I don't think a man has the right to slave-drive his wife just because she is a woman. A man who doesn't want his wife to work after the war isn't trying to make her a servant. The wife-and-mother job is one to be respected. It takes real brains and imagination to keep a home running smoothly and to bring up children that you can be proud of.... Being a mother is a real profession, with a lot of dignity and satisfaction about it if you look at it right. A woman who tries to hire a substitute homemaker may have to pay as much as she makes herself and then not get the real thing."

"Look, Con," says Pro, "You are still overworking this motherhood stuff. Maybe you didn't know about it, but children do grow up and furthermore a woman doesn't have them all her life. If she builds her life around children and nothing else, she is going to be left pretty flat when they grow up and leave home. If she has gotten used to thinking about nothing else but her kids she won't believe that they have grown up. She may try to hang on to them, boss them around, and make a general nuisance of herself. The really nasty

---

[1] Nazi doctrine held that women should be wives and mothers and not be involved in politics.

mothers-in-law are the ones that don't have enough to do. If a woman has a job to keep her occupied after her children are grown up she's doing something useful and is likely to mind her own business."

Pvt. Con breaks in, "Pro, you certainly do like to put women to work. I bet you wouldn't mind going home after the war and sending your own mother out to run a blast furnace. Women just aren't suited to work outside the home in the same way a man does. It takes a lot out of them to bear children. They need to be protected. By the time a woman has brought up a flock of kids she deserves a rest. There's plenty to do around the home. If she's taken the job of motherhood seriously and knows how to do it right she can help out with the grandchildren when they come thick and fast. If some women must go out and work, it should be the young unmarried ones that are now paid to take care of children. Let the housemaids work in the factories and let the grandmothers make some use of their experience in the home."

Pvt. Pro objects, "Con, you talk as though a married woman could always count on a husband's pay check, and that isn't so. A married woman needs the extra protection that comes with a job or at least the chance to get one. Then she doesn't have all her eggs in the same basket. If her marriage cracks up, she's got something to fall back on and doesn't have to depend on the skimpy alimony which even the sheriff may not be able to collect. Even if a marriage turns out all right the husband is going to get old and may lose his job. A lot of young husbands were walking the streets during the depression. Then there is the chance at any age that the husband may die. If the widow has a job and is used to working, she is in a lot better position to carry on."

Pvt. Con snorts, "Didn't you ever hear of insurance, Pro? Where were you when they were peddling the ten thousand dollar government policies? If a woman is an economical housekeeper her husband can afford to take out insurance which will take care of her if he kicks off. Sure, I know all about the depression. I peddled papers during a good part of it, but depressions aren't necessary. When this social security business gets worked out a little bit more the family is going to be protected."

Document 31

Potsdam Declaration
July 26, 1945

Germany surrendered on May 7, 1945, but Allied leaders did not meet until July to decide how to handle the transition to peace. They gathered in Potsdam, Germany, just outside Berlin, from July 17–August 2, 1945. The major Allied delegations were led by US President Harry S. Truman – who as Vice President had become president upon the death of Franklin Roosevelt on April 12, 1945 – British Prime Minister Winston Churchill, and Soviet leader Joseph Stalin. The Allies agreed to separate Germany and Berlin into four zones, each controlled by a different Allied nation (France, Britain, USSR, and the United States). Germany was also required to disarm completely. During the war, the Allies had called for Germany's unconditional surrender, and the Potsdam Conference decided what "unconditional surrender" meant.

Meanwhile, the war in the Pacific continued. On July 16, 1945, a day before the Potsdam conference began, President Truman received word that the United States had successfully detonated an atomic bomb in the New Mexico desert. Truman took advantage of the meeting in Potsdam to issue a joint statement (with Britain and the Republic of China; the Soviet Union did not sign because it had not declared war on Japan) demanding Japan's unconditional surrender. The Potsdam Declaration also outlined what continuing the war – or, alternatively, what peace – would mean for Japan.

Source: Proclamation Defining Terms for Japanese Surrender, Issued, at Potsdam, July 26, 1945 (Birth of the Constitution of Japan, National Diet Library, Japan) https://goo.gl/vk6tQV.

Proclamation Defining Terms for Japanese Surrender
Issued, at Potsdam, July 26, 1945

1. We – the President of the United States, the President of the National Government of the Republic of China, and the Prime Minister of Great Britain, representing the hundreds of millions of our

countrymen, have conferred and agree that Japan shall be given an opportunity to end this war.

2. The prodigious land, sea and air forces of the United States, the British Empire and of China, many times reinforced by their armies and air fleets from the west, are poised to strike the final blows upon Japan. This military power is sustained and inspired by the determination of all the Allied Nations to prosecute the war against Japan until she ceases to resist.

3. The result of the futile and senseless German resistance to the might of the aroused free peoples of the world stands forth in awful clarity as an example to the people of Japan. The might that now converges on Japan is immeasurably greater than that which, when applied to the resisting Nazis, necessarily laid waste to the lands, the industry and the method of life of the whole German people. The full application of our military power, backed by our resolve, will mean the inevitable and complete destruction of the Japanese armed forces and just as inevitably the utter devastation of the Japanese homeland.

4. The time has come for Japan to decide whether she will continue to be controlled by those self-willed militaristic advisers whose unintelligent calculations have brought the Empire of Japan to the threshold of annihilation, or whether she will follow the path of reason.

5. Following are our terms. We will not deviate from them. There are no alternatives. We shall brook no delay.

6. There must be eliminated for all time the authority and influence of those who have deceived and misled the people of Japan into embarking on world conquest, for we insist that a new order of peace, security and justice will be impossible until irresponsible militarism is driven from the world.

7. Until such a new order is established and until there is convincing proof that Japan's war-making power is destroyed, points in Japanese territory to be designated by the Allies shall be occupied to secure the achievement of the basic objectives we are here setting forth.

8. The terms of the Cairo Declaration shall be carried out and Japanese sovereignty shall be limited to the islands of Honshu, Hokkaido, Kyushu, Shikoku and such minor islands as we determine.[1]
9. The Japanese military forces, after being completely disarmed, shall be permitted to return to their homes with the opportunity to lead peaceful and productive lives.
10. We do not intend that the Japanese shall be enslaved as a race or destroyed as a nation, but stern justice shall be meted out to all war criminals, including those who have visited cruelties upon our prisoners. The Japanese Government shall remove all obstacles to the revival and strengthening of democratic tendencies among the Japanese people. Freedom of speech, of religion, and of thought, as well as respect for the fundamental human rights shall be established.
11. Japan shall be permitted to maintain such industries as will sustain her economy and permit the exaction of just reparations in kind, but not those which would enable her to re-arm for war. To this end, access to, as distinguished from control of, raw materials shall be permitted. Eventual Japanese participation in world trade relations shall be permitted.
12. The occupying forces of the Allies shall be withdrawn from Japan as soon as these objectives have been accomplished and there has been established in accordance with the freely expressed will of the Japanese people a peacefully inclined and responsible government.
13. We call upon the government of Japan to proclaim now the unconditional surrender of all Japanese armed forces, and to provide proper and adequate assurances of their good faith in such action. The alternative for Japan is prompt and utter destruction.

---

[1] In the 1943 Cairo Declaration, the United States, Britain, and China had pledged to eject Japanese forces from all conquered lands, including China, Korea, and Pacific Islands.

Document 32

Press Release Alerting the Nation About the Atomic Bomb

Harry S. Truman
August 6, 1945

The final year of the Pacific war was bloody. Japanese kamikaze attacks on ships and the tenacity of Japanese ground troops on Pacific islands raised U.S. casualties. The US also increased the number and intensity of conventional bombing attacks on Japan. The most devastating came on March 9–10, 1945 when bombs leveled nearly 16 square miles in Tokyo and killed 90,000 Japanese.

On August 6, 1945, the United States dropped an atomic bomb on Hiroshima, Japan, killing 80,000 people instantly. The bomb was the culmination of a four-year secret project to build a nuclear weapon, known as the Manhattan Project. Most of the country learned about the new weapon from this White House press release. Three days later, the United States dropped a second atomic bomb on Nagasaki that killed 35,000 people. Japan surrendered on August 14, 1945.

Source: Press Release by the White House, August 6, 1945 (Ayers Papers, U. S. Army Press Releases, Harry S. Truman Library). https://goo.gl/KPQHMW

THE WHITE HOUSE
Washington, D.C.
STATEMENT BY THE PRESIDENT OF THE UNITED STATES

Sixteen hours ago an American airplane dropped one bomb on Hiroshima and destroyed its usefulness to the enemy. That bomb had more power than 20,000 tons of TNT. It had more than two thousand times the blast power of the British "Grand Slam" which is the largest bomb ever yet used in the history of warfare.

The Japanese began the war from the air at Pearl Harbor. They have been repaid manyfold. And the end is not yet. With this bomb we have now added a new and revolutionary increase in destruction to supplement the growing power of our armed forces. In their present form these bombs are now in production and even more powerful forms are in development.

It is an atomic bomb. It is a harnessing of the basic power of the universe. The force from which the sun draws its power has been loosed against those who brought war to the Far East.

Before 1939, it was the accepted belief of scientists that it was theoretically possible to release atomic energy. But no one knew any practical method of doing it. By 1942, however, we knew that the Germans were working feverishly to find a way to add atomic energy to the other engines of war with which they hoped to enslave the world. But they failed. We may be grateful to Providence that the Germans got the V-1's and V-2's late and in limited quantities and even more grateful that they did not get the atomic bomb at all.

The battle of the laboratories held fateful risks for us as well as the battles of the air, land, and sea, and we have now won the battle of the laboratories as we have won the other battles.

Beginning in 1940, before Pearl Harbor, scientific knowledge useful in war was pooled between the United States and Great Britain, and many priceless helps to our victories have come from that arrangement. Under that general policy the research on the atomic bomb was begun. With American and British scientists working together we entered the race of discovery against the Germans.

The United States had available the large number of scientists of distinction in the many needed areas of knowledge. It had the tremendous industrial and financial resources necessary for the project and they could be devoted to it without undue impairment of other vital war work. In the United States the laboratory work and the production plants, on which a substantial start had already been made, would be out of reach of enemy bombing, while at that time Britain was exposed to constant air attack and was still threatened with the possibility of invasion. For these reasons Prime Minister Churchill and President Roosevelt agreed that it was wise to carry on the project here.

We now have two great plants and many lesser works devoted to the production of atomic power. Employment during peak construction numbered 125,000 and over 65,000 individuals are even now engaged in operating the plants. Many have worked there for two and a half years. Few know what they have been producing. They see great quantities of material going in and they see nothing coming out of these plants, for the physical size of the explosive charge is exceedingly small. We have spent two billion dollars on the greatest scientific gamble in history – and won.

But the greatest marvel is not the size of the enterprise, its secrecy, nor its cost, but the achievement of scientific brains in putting together infinitely complex pieces of knowledge held by many men in different fields of science into a workable plan. And hardly less marvelous has been the capacity of industry to design and of labor to operate, the machines and methods to do things never done before so that the brainchild of many minds came forth in physical shape and performed as it was supposed to do. Both science and industry worked under the direction of the United States Army, which achieved a unique success in managing so diverse a problem in the advancement of knowledge in an amazingly short time. It is doubtful if such another combination could be got together in the world. What has been done is the greatest achievement of organized science in history. It was done under pressure and without failure.

We are now prepared to obliterate more rapidly and completely every productive enterprise the Japanese have above ground in any city. We shall destroy their docks, their factories, and their communications. Let there be no mistake; we shall completely destroy Japan's power to make war.

It was to spare the Japanese people from utter destruction that the ultimatum of July 26 was issued at Potsdam.[1] Their leaders promptly rejected that ultimatum. If they do not now accept our terms they may expect a rain of ruin from the air, the like of which has never been seen on this earth. Behind this air attack will follow sea and land forces in such number and power as they have not yet seen and with the fighting skill of which they are already well aware.

The Secretary of War, who has kept in personal touch with all phases of the project, will immediately make public a statement giving further details.

His statement will give facts concerning the sites at Oak Ridge near Knoxville, Tennessee, and at Richland, near Pasco, Washington, and an installation near Santa Fe, New Mexico. Although the workers at the sites have been making materials to be used producing the greatest destructive force in history they have not themselves been in danger beyond that of many other occupations, for the utmost care has been taken of their safety.[2]

---

[1] See Document 31.
[2] Researchers from the Los Alamos Historical Document Retrieval and Assessment project being led by the Centers for Disease Control and Prevention (CDC) would report in 2007 that civilians living near the test site in the White Sands desert of New Mexico were exposed to high levels of radiation.

The fact that we can release atomic energy ushers in a new era in man's understanding of nature's forces. Atomic energy may in the future supplement the power that now comes from coal, oil, and falling water, but at present it cannot be produced on a basis to compete with them commercially. Before that comes there must be a long period of intensive research. It has never been the habit of the scientists of this country or the policy of this government to withhold from the world scientific knowledge. Normally, therefore, everything about the work with atomic energy would be made public.

But under the present circumstances it is not intended to divulge the technical processes of production or all the military applications, pending further examination of possible methods of protecting us and the rest of the world from the danger of sudden destruction.

I shall recommend that the Congress of the United States consider promptly the establishment of an appropriate commission to control the production and use of atomic power within the United States. I shall give further consideration and make further recommendations to the Congress as to how atomic power can become a powerful and forceful influence towards the maintenance of world peace.

Document 33

The Effects of Atomic Bombs on Hiroshima and Nagasaki
United States Strategic Bombing Survey
July 1, 1946

In World War II, the United States and Britain executed massive aerial bombing attacks on European cities. The initial goal was strategic bombing – destroying industrial, manufacturing, and transportation facilities while sparing civilian areas. These distinctions gradually broke down during the war, especially when the US began bombing Japanese cities with conventional weapons. By the time the United States dropped the atomic bomb on Hiroshima, efforts to separate military from civilian targets had ceased.

The War Department created the United States Strategic Bombing Survey *to evaluate the effectiveness of these various bombing campaigns in Europe and the Pacific, including the physical devastation caused by dropping atomic bombs on Hiroshima and Nagasaki. Besides assessing the damage to Japan, the report also suggested that the data collected would be useful in helping the United States defend its cities in the future from nuclear attack. The following excerpt is taken from the conclusion of the report. We can see in it the germ of the civil defense efforts in the United States in the 1950s and 1960s.*

Source: Chapter IV: "Signposts," United States Strategic Bombing Survey *(Government Printing Office: Washington, D.C., 1946), p. 36 – 43. https://goo.gl/WZvcgG*

A. The Danger

The Survey's investigators, as they proceeded about their study, sound an insistent question framing itself in their minds: "What if the target for the bomb had been an American City?" True, the primary mission of the Survey was to ascertain the facts just summarized. But conclusions as to the meaning of those facts, for citizens of the United States, forced themselves almost inescapably on the men who examined thoughtfully the remains of Hiroshima and Nagasaki....

B. What Can We Do About It

The danger is real – of that, the Survey's findings leave no doubt. Scattered through those findings, at the same time, are the clues to the measures that can be taken to cut down potential losses of lives and property. These measures must be taken or initiated now, if their cost is not to be prohibitive. But if a policy is laid down, well in advance of any crisis, it will enable timely decentralization of industrial and medical facilities, construction or blueprinting of shelters, and preparation for life-saving evacuation programs. The almost unprotected, completely surprised cities of Japan suffered maximum losses from atomic bomb attack. If we recognize in advance the possible danger and act to forestall it, we shall at worst suffer minimum casualties and disruption.

Since modern science can be marshalled for the defense as well as the attack, there is reason to hope that protective weapons and techniques will be improved. Even protective devices and vigilance, however, cannot be perfect guards against surprise or initial attack, or against the unlimited choices of targets offered an enemy through the range and speed of modern weapons. In our planning for the future, if we are realistic, we will prepare to minimize the destructiveness of such attacks, and so organize the economic and administrative life of the Nation that no single or small group of successful attacks can paralyze the national organism. The foregoing description of the effectiveness of the atomic bomb has shown clearly that, despite its awesome power, it has limits of which wise planning will take prompt advantage.

1. Shelters

The most instructive fact at Nagasaki was the survival, even when near ground zero, of the few hundred people who were properly placed in the tunnel shelters. Carefully built shelters, though unoccupied, stood up well in both cities. Without question, shelters can protect those who get to them against anything but a direct hit. Adequate warning will assure that a maximum number get to shelters.

Analysis of the protection of survivors within a few hundred feet of ground zero shows that shielding is possible even against gamma rays. At Hiroshima, for example, persons in a concrete building 3,600 feet from ground zero showed no clinical effects from gamma radiation, but those protected only by wooden buildings at a similar distance suffered from radiation disease. The necessary thickness varies with the substance and with the distance from the point of detonation. Adequate shelters can be built which will reduce substantially the casualties from radiation.

Men arriving at Hiroshima and Nagasaki have been constantly impressed by the shells of reinforced concrete buildings still rising above the rubble of brick and stone or the ashes of wooden buildings. In most cases gutted by fire or stripped of partitions and interior trim, these buildings have a double lesson for us. They show, first, that it is possible without excessive expense to erect buildings which will satisfactorily protect their contents at distances of about 2,000 feet or more from a bomb of the types so far employed. Construction of such buildings would be similar to earthquake resistant construction, which California experience indicates would cost about 10 percent to 15 percent more than conventional construction. Even against more powerful bombs or against near misses, such construction would diminish damage. Second, the internal damage illustrates the danger from interior details and construction which result in fire or flying debris in otherwise sound buildings. The elimination of combustible interiors and the provision of full-masonry partition walls, fire-resistive stair and elevator enclosures, and fire division walls would localize fires....

. . . .

3. Civilian Defense

Because the scale of disaster would be certain to overwhelm the locality in which it occurs, mutual assistance organized on a national level is essential. Such national organization is by no means inconsistent with decentralization; indeed, it will be aided by the existence of the maximum number of nearly self-sustaining regions whose joint support it can coordinate. In addition, highly trained mobile units skilled in and equipped for fire-fighting, rescue work, and clearance and repair should be trained for an emergency which disrupts local organization and exceeds its capability for control.

Most important, a national civilian defense organization can prepare now the plans for necessary steps in case of crisis. Two complementary programs which should be worked out in advance are those for evacuation of unnecessary inhabitants from threatened urban areas, and for rapid erection of adequate shelters for people who must remain.

4. Active Defense

Protective measures can substantially reduce the degree of devastation from an atomic bomb and the rate of casualties. Yet if the possibility of atomic attack on us is accepted, we must accept also the fact that no defensive measures alone can long protect us. At best they can minimize our losses and preserve the functioning of the national community through initial or continuing partial attack. Against full and sustained attacks they would be ineffectual palliatives.

As defensive weapons, atomic bombs are useful primarily as warnings, as threats of retaliation which will restrain a potential aggressor from their use as from the use of poison gas or biological warfare. The mission of active defense, as of passive defense, is thus to prevent the surprise use of the atomic bomb from being decisive. A wise military establishment will make sure – by dispersal, concealment, protection, and constant readiness of its forces – that no single blow or series of blows from an enemy can cripple its ability to strike back in the same way or to repel accompanying attacks from other air, ground, or sea forces. The measures to enable this unrelaxing state of readiness are not new; only their urgency is increased. Particularly is this true of the intelligence activities on which informed decisions and timely actions depend.

The need for research is not limited to atomic energy itself, but is equally important in propellants, detection devices, and other techniques of countering and of delivering atomic weapons. Also imperative is the testing of the weapon's potentialities under varying conditions. The coming Operation Crossroads,[1] for example, will give valuable data for defining more precisely what is already known about the atomic bomb's effectiveness when air-burst; more valuable, however, will be tests under new conditions, to provide sure information about detonations at water level or under water, as well as underground. While prediction of effects under differing conditions of detonation may have a high degree of probability, verified knowledge is a much better basis for military planning.

5. Conclusion

One further measure of safety must accompany the others. To avoid destruction, the surest way is to avoid war. This was the Survey's

---

[1] Nuclear weapons tests carried out at Bikini atoll in 1946

recommendation after viewing the rubble of German cities, and it holds equally true whether one remembers the ashes of Hiroshima or considers the vulnerability of American cities.

Our national policy has consistently had as one of its basic principles the maintenance of peace. Based on our ideals of justice and of peaceful development of our resources, this disinterested policy has been reinforced by our clear lack of anything to gain from war – even in victory. No more forceful arguments for peace and for the international machinery of peace than the sight of the devastation of Hiroshima and Nagasaki have ever been devised. As the developer and exploiter of this ominous weapon, our nation has a responsibility, which no American should shirk, to lead in establishing and implementing the international guarantees and controls which will prevent its future use.

Document 34

Report on the Nuremberg Trials
Justice Robert H. Jackson
October 7, 1946

In 1945 and 1946 the Allies jointly tried 22 Nazi leaders in the Nuremberg War Crimes Trial. Justice Robert H. Jackson took a leave of absence from the Supreme Court to serve as U.S. Chief of Counsel for the American delegation. The person most responsible for the Holocaust was already dead when the trials took place. Adolph Hitler had committed suicide just before Soviet troops entered Berlin in April 1945. Many other Nazi officials followed his lead or fled the country in secret to avoid prosecution. Jackson sent this report to President Harry S. Truman at the conclusion of the trials, which he judged a success. Tracking down and prosecuting Nazi war criminals, however, continued for decades after the war. The United States also convened war crimes trials throughout East Asia, trying 28 major Japanese leaders.

Source: *Report of Robert H. Jackson, United States Representative to the International Conference on Military Trials* (U. S. Department of State, Publication 3080, February 1949). https://goo.gl/nykaer

---

October 7, 1946

THE PRESIDENT, The White House, Washington, D. C.

MY DEAR MR. PRESIDENT:

I have the honor to report as to the duties which you delegated to me on May 2, 1945 in connection with the prosecution of major Nazi war criminals.

The International Military Tribunal sitting at Nurnberg,[1] Germany on 30 September and 1 October, 1946 rendered judgment in the first international criminal assizes in history. It found 19 of the 22 defendants guilty on one or more of the counts of the Indictment, and acquitted 3. It sentenced 12 to death

---

[1] Nurnberg is the German name for Nuremberg.

by hanging, 3 to imprisonment for life, and the four others to terms of 10 to 20 years imprisonment....

In preparation for the trial over 100,000 captured German documents were screened or examined and about 10,000 were selected for intensive examination as having probable evidentiary value. Of these, about 4,000 were translated into four languages and used, in whole or in part, in the trial as exhibits. Millions of feet of captured moving picture film were examined and over 100,000 feet brought to Nurnberg. Relevant sections were prepared and introduced as exhibits. Over 25,000 captured still photographs were brought to Nurnberg, together with Hitler's personal photographer who took most of them. More than 1,800 were selected and prepared for use as exhibits. The Tribunal, in its judgment, states: "The case, therefore, against the defendants rests in large measure on documents of their own making, the authenticity of which has not been challenged except in one or two cases." The English translations of most of the documents are now being published by the Departments of State and War in eight volumes and will be a valuable and permanent source for the war history....

Although my personal undertaking is at an end, any report would be incomplete and misleading which failed to take account of the general war crimes work that remains undone and the heavy burden that falls to successors in this work. A very large number of Germans who have participated in the crimes remain unpunished. There are many industrialists, militarists, politicians, diplomats, and police officials whose guilt does not differ from those who have been convicted except that their parts were at lower levels and have been less conspicuous....

The importance of the trial lies in the principles to which the Four Powers became committed by the Agreement, by their participation in the prosecution, and by the judgment rendered by the Tribunal. What has been accomplished may be summarized as follows:

1. We negotiated and concluded an Agreement with the four dominant powers of the earth, signed at London on August 8, 1945, which for the first time made explicit and unambiguous what was theretofore, as the Tribunal has declared, implicit in International Law, namely, that to prepare, incite, or wage a war of aggression, or to conspire with others to do so, is a crime against international society, and that to persecute, oppress, or do violence to individuals or minorities on political, racial, or religious grounds in connection with such a war, or to exterminate, enslave, or deport civilian populations, is an international crime, and that for the commission of such crimes individuals are responsible. This agreement also won the adherence of nineteen additional

nations and represents the combined judgments of the overwhelming majority of civilized people. It is a basic charter in the International Law of the future.

2. We have also incorporated its principles into a judicial precedent. "The power of the precedent," Mr. Justice Cardozo[2] said, "is the power of the beaten path." One of the chief obstacles to this trial was the lack of a beaten path. A judgment such as has been rendered shifts the power of the precedent to the support of these rules of law. No one can hereafter deny or fail to know that the principles on which the Nazi leaders are adjudged to forfeit their lives constitute law and law with a sanction.

3. The Agreement devised a workable procedure for the trial of crimes which reconciled the basic conflicts in Anglo-American, French, and Soviet procedures.... It would be idle to pretend that we have not had moments of difference and vexation, but the steadfast purpose of all delegations that this first international trial should prove the possibility of successful international cooperation in use of the litigation process, always overcame transient irritations.

4. In a world torn with hatreds and suspicions where passions are stirred by the "frantic boast and foolish word," the Four Powers have given the example of submitting their grievances against these men to a dispassionate inquiry on legal evidence.... It is not too much to hope that this example of full and fair hearing, and tranquil and discriminating judgment will do something toward strengthening the processes of justice in many countries.

5. We have documented from German sources the Nazi aggressions, persecutions, and atrocities with such authenticity and in such detail that there can be no responsible denial of these crimes in the future and no tradition of martyrdom of the Nazi leaders can arise among informed people. No history of this era can be entitled to authority which fails to take into account the record of Nurnberg. While an effort was made by Goering and others to portray themselves as "glowing patriots," their admitted crimes of violence and meanness, of greed and graft, leave no ground for future admiration of their characters and their fate leaves no incentive to emulation of their examples.[3]

6. It has been well said that this trial is the world's first post mortem examination of a totalitarian regime. In this trial, the Nazis themselves with Machiavellian shamelessness exposed their methods of subverting people's

---

[2] Benjamin Cardozo was an Associate Justice of the Supreme Court from 1932 until his death in 1938.

[3] Hermann Goering (1893–1946), founder of the Gestapo, the German secret political police, and highest-ranking Nazi official tried at Nuremberg.

liberties and establishing their dictatorship. The record is a merciless exposé of the cruel and sordid methods by which a militant minority seized power, suppressed opposition, set up secret political police and concentration camps. They resorted to legal devices such as "protective custody," which Goering frankly said meant the arrest of people not because they had committed any crime but because of acts it was suspected they might commit if left at liberty. They destroyed all judicial remedies for the citizen and all protections against terrorism. The record discloses the early symptoms of dictatorship and shows that it is only in its incipient stages that it can be brought under control. And the testimony records the German example that the destruction of opposition produces eventual deterioration in the government that does it. By progressive intolerance a dictatorship by its very nature becomes so arbitrary that it cannot tolerate opposition, even when it consists merely of the correction of misinformation or the communication to its highest officers of unwelcome intelligence. It was really the recoil of the Nazi blows at liberty that destroyed the Nazi regime. They struck down freedom of speech and press and other freedoms which pass as ordinary civil rights with us, so thoroughly that not even its highest officers dared to warn the people or the Fuehrer that they were taking the road to destruction. The Nurnberg trial has put that handwriting on the wall for the oppressor as well as the oppressed to read.

Of course, it would be extravagant to claim that agreements or trials of this character can make aggressive war or persecution of minorities impossible, just as it would be extravagant to claim that our federal laws make federal crime impossible. But we cannot doubt that they strengthen the bulwarks of peace and tolerance. The four nations through their prosecutors and through their representatives on the Tribunal, have enunciated standards of conduct which bring new hope to men of good will and from which future statesmen will not lightly depart. These standards by which the Germans have been condemned will become the condemnation of any nation that is faithless to them.

By the Agreement and this trial we have put International Law squarely on the side of peace as against aggressive warfare, and on the side of humanity as against persecution. In the present depressing world outlook it is possible that the Nurnberg trial may constitute the most important moral advance to grow out of this war. The trial and decision by which the four nations have forfeited the lives of some of the most powerful political and military leaders of Germany because they have violated fundamental International Law, does more than anything in our time to give to International Law what Woodrow

Wilson described as "the kind of vitality it can only have if it is a real expression of our moral judgment."[4]

I hereby resign my commission as your representative and Chief of Counsel for the United States. In its execution I have had the help of many able men and women, too many to mention individually, who have made personal sacrifice to carry on a work in which they earnestly believed. I also want to express deep personal appreciation for this opportunity to do what I believe to be a constructive work for the peace of the world and for the better protection of persecuted peoples. It was, perhaps, the greatest opportunity ever presented to an American lawyer. In pursuit of it many mistakes have been made and many inadequacies must be confessed. I am consoled by the fact that in proceedings of this novelty, errors and missteps may also be instructive to the future.

Respectfully submitted,
ROBERT H. JACKSON

---

[4] In a speech on May 9, 1919 to the International Law Society in Paris.

Appendices

Appendix A:
Thematic Table of Contents

US Neutrality

1. Neutrality Act of 1935 (August 31, 1935)
2. Bennett Champ Clark, A Senator Defends the First Neutrality Act (December 1935)
3. Franklin D. Roosevelt, President Roosevelt Defends Lend-Lease (December 17, 1940)
4. Franklin D. Roosevelt, "Arsenal of Democracy" Fireside Chat (December 29, 1940)
5. Franklin D. Roosevelt, "The Four Freedoms" (January 6, 1941)
6. Gallup Polls (January 1940 – January 1941)
8. Charles Lindbergh, "America First" (April 23, 1941)
11. Franklin D. Roosevelt, Fireside Chat on the *Greer* Incident (September 11, 1941)
12. Robert A. Taft, "Repeal of Neutrality Act Means War" (October 28, 1941)
13. Gallup Polls (April – October 1941)

Entering the War

14. Claude R. Wickard, Reacting to Pearl Harbor (December 7, 1941)
15. Franklin D. Roosevelt, "A Date Which Will Live in Infamy" (December 8, 1941)

African Americans and the Double-Victory Campaign

7. Eleanor Roosevelt, The First Lady Visits Tuskegee (April 1, 1941)
9. Franklin D. Roosevelt, Executive Order 8802 – Prohibition of Discrimination in the Defense Industry (June 25, 1941)
20. A. Philip Randolph, "Why Should We March?" (November 1942)
21. Franklin D. Roosevelt, Executive Order 9346 - Establishing a Committee on Fair Employment Practice (May 27, 1943)

24. Corporal Rupert Trimmingham's Letters to *Yank* Magazine (April 28, 1944 and July 28, 1944)

Japanese-American Internment

16. Franklin D. Roosevelt, Executive Order 9066 – Resulting in the Relocation of Japanese (February 19, 1942)
17. Japanese-American Evacuation (April – May, 1942)
27. Ansel Adams, Manzanar: Excerpt from *Born Free and Equal* (1944)
29. *Korematsu v. US* (December 18, 1944)

On the Battlefront

19. James Fahey, *Pacific War Diary* (1942 – 1945)
23. Ernie Pyle, "The Death of Captain Waskow" (January 10, 1944)
25. Dwight D. Eisenhower, D-Day Statement to the Allied Expeditionary Force (June 5 – 6, 1944)
28. General Douglas MacArthur, Radio Address Upon Returning to the Philippines (October 20, 1944)

Women

22. United States Army Women's Auxiliary Corps, Questions and Answers About the WAAC (1943)
30. G.I. Roundtable Series, "Do You Want Your Wife to Work After the War?" (1944)

The Holocaust

18. First news of the Final Solution (August 10 – 11, 1942)
26. Stopping the Holocaust (August 9 and August 14, 1944)
34. Justice Robert H. Jackson, *Report on the Nuremburg Trials* (October 7, 1946)

The Atomic Bomb

31. Potsdam Declaration (July 26, 1945)

32. Harry S. Truman, Press Release Alerting the Nation About the Atomic Bomb (August 6, 1945)

33. United States Strategic Bombing Survey, *The Effects of Atomic Bombs on Hiroshima and Nagasaki* (July 1, 1946)

Appendix B:
Study Questions

For each of the Documents in this collection, we suggest below in section A questions relevant for that document alone and in Section B questions that require comparison between documents.

1. Neutrality Act of 1935 (August 31, 1935)

A. What actions did the Neutrality Act specifically prohibit? How were such restrictions meant to protect American neutrality? What potential problems might arise with these restrictions?

B. On what grounds did Senator Bennett Champ Clark argue in Document 2 that this first Neutrality Act was insufficient?

2. Bennett Champ Clark, A Senator Defends the First Neutrality Act (December 1935)

A. What conclusions did Clark draw from the nation's experience in World War I? How did he characterize the munitions industry in the United States? What steps did he believe the United States must take to maintain strict neutrality?

B. How is Clark's negative view of the impact of war on American society echoed in Charles Lindbergh's 1941 "America First" address (Document 8)?

3. Franklin D. Roosevelt, President Roosevelt Defends Lend-Lease (December 17, 1940)

A. How did Roosevelt characterize Lend-Lease in these remarks to the press? How did he characterize America's experience in World War I?

B. Both Senator Clark (Document 2) and President Roosevelt claimed that they wanted to avoid fighting another war. What different approaches did they take to meeting that goal?

Study Questions

4. Franklin D. Roosevelt, "Arsenal of Democracy" Fireside Chat (December 29, 1940)

A. Why, according to Roosevelt, do the Atlantic and Pacific Oceans no longer guarantee the safety of the United States? How did he characterize non-interventionists and the "America First" movement? Why were the Nazis a unique threat to world civilization? How did Roosevelt propose that the United States help Great Britain?

B. Are Roosevelt's proposals in keeping with the spirit of the Neutrality Acts (Documents 1 and 2)?

5. Franklin D. Roosevelt, "The Four Freedoms" (January 6, 1941)

A. What are the Four Freedoms? According to Roosevelt, how do they define the "democratic way of life" in the United States? What connections did Roosevelt make in this speech between his domestic and foreign policies?

B. Consider this speech alongside Roosevelt's press conference on Lend-Lease (Document 3) and his Arsenal of Democracy fireside chat (Document 4). How did Roosevelt build a coherent foreign policy through his various addresses to the nation?

6. Gallup Polls (January 1940 – January 1941)

A. How did Americans' views change over time about the likelihood of the United States entering World War II? Did the questions Gallup asked shape the responses given? What accounts for these shifting views?

B. Consider the polls before and after Roosevelt's Lend-Lease proposal (Document 3) on December 17, 1940 and his Arsenal of Democracy Speech (Document 4) on December 29, 1940. To what extent was Roosevelt constrained by these polls? In what respects was he responding to these polls? How was he shaping public opinion? Lend-Lease was approved in March 1941. Consider these same questions for the polls before and after its approval (Document 13).

7. Eleanor Roosevelt, The First Lady Visits Tuskegee (April 1, 1941)

A. What accomplishments at Tuskegee did Eleanor Roosevelt highlight, and why did she emphasize these particular accomplishments? What message did she send by having her photograph taken before her airplane ride?

B. How does Tuskegee's approach to improving the lives of African Americans compare to the tactics of the March on Washington Movement (Document 20)?

8. Charles Lindbergh, "America First" (April 23, 1941)

A. Why did Lindbergh believe that the United States would lose if it decided to enter the European War? Why did he call his recommendation a policy of independence, not isolationism? What did Lindbergh mean when he said, "Practically every difficulty we would face in invading Europe becomes an asset to us in defending America."

B. Compare this speech to Roosevelt's "Arsenal of Democracy" speech (Document 4). How does Lindbergh's view of how oceans impact national security differ from Roosevelt's perspective? What actions did each speaker encourage on the part of the general public? Is there something especially "democratic" about either or both appeals?

9. Franklin D. Roosevelt, Executive Order 8802 – Prohibition of Discrimination in the Defense Industry (June 25, 1941)

A. What measures did Executive Order 8802 prescribe to address racial prejudice? What problems did it not address?

B. How did Executive Order 8802 strengthen the claims that FDR made about democracy in the Four Freedoms address (Document 5) and the Atlantic Charter (Document 10)?

10. The Atlantic Charter (August 14, 1941)

A. What type of partnership did the Atlantic Charter create between the United States and Great Britain?

B. How are the themes of Roosevelt's Four Freedoms speech (Document 5) reiterated in the Atlantic Charter? What objections might members of the "America First" Movement (Document 8) make to the Atlantic Charter?

11. Franklin D. Roosevelt, Fireside Chat on the *Greer* Incident (September 11, 1941)

A. Why should Americans care about the *Greer* attack, according to Roosevelt? What did he believe would happen to the United States in a Nazi-dominated world? Why did he reject a strategy of diplomacy and appeasement?

B. How did Roosevelt address the likely objections of non-interventionists like Lindbergh (Document 8) in explaining his decision to protect merchant ships from other nations?

12. Robert A. Taft, "Repeal of Neutrality Act Means War" (October 28, 1941)

A. What objections does Taft raise to Roosevelt's exercise of executive power in his foreign policy? Which policies is he specifically criticizing? Why isn't he concerned about shifts in public opinion?

B. According to Gallup poll results, how popular are Taft's views in 1940? In 1941? (Documents 6 and 13)? What counter argument does Roosevelt present in his *Greer* incident speech (Document 11)?

13. Gallup Polls (April – October 1941)

A. How would you characterize the state of American public opinion concerning the war in Europe in the months before Pearl Harbor? What changes after the *Greer* incident in September 1941?

B. Are there significant differences in public opinion in 1941, as compared to 1940 (Document 6)? After the *Greer* incident (Document 11), how much public support does FDR have for his foreign policies?

14. Claude Wickard, Reacting to Pearl Harbor (December 7, 1941)

A. How would you characterize the reactions of Roosevelt and other government officials in the immediate aftermath of the attack on Pearl Harbor? What questions immediately arose?

B. How does this private conversation compare with the public address Roosevelt gave the next day in his "Day of Infamy" Speech before Congress (Document 15)?

15. Franklin D. Roosevelt, "A Date Which Will Live in Infamy" (December 8, 1941)

A. What are the key points that Roosevelt wanted to convey in this brief address? Why did he focus exclusively on Japan, and not mention Germany at all?

B. How did Roosevelt indirectly address the concerns of non-interventionists like Charles Lindbergh (Document 8) in his speech?

16. Franklin D. Roosevelt, Executive Order No. 9066 – Resulting in the Relocation of Japanese (February 19, 1942)

A. What did the EO 9066 authorize? Why did it not mention Japanese Americans by name? Did the order establish internment camps?

B. How did the Supreme Court reaffirm the powers that EO 9066 gave military commanders to issue exclusion orders (Document 29)?

17. Japanese-American Evacuation (April – May, 1942)

A. How much time were residents given to prepare for departure? What rules governed how much they could bring? What message does Lange's photograph convey about the motivations behind the evacuation? Why would Lange photograph the exclusion order posted alongside air raid instructions? Does seeing the poster alone offer a different interpretation of the exclusion order?

B. What happened to Toyosaburo Korematsu (Document 29) when he failed to leave the excluded area? Why did he stay?

18. First news of the Final Solution (August 10 – 11, 1942)

A. How did Harrison's reaction to the report of German plans to exterminate Jews differ from Elting's reaction? How did each justify his reaction?

B. What key decisions did the United States make in responding to the Holocaust (Documents 26 and 34)?

Study Questions 177

19. James Fahey, *Pacific War Diary* (1942 – 1945)

A. How do Fahey's views of the Japanese change during the course of his military service? What factors shaped his views during and after the war? How did Fahey's combat experience shape his views of the Japanese? What key observations does he make about the character of the war in the Pacific? How does he explain men's willingness to fight?

B. What is Fahey's account of MacArthur's return to the Philippines (Document 28)? What perspective do these two accounts give on the war in the Pacific?

20. A. Philip Randolph, "Why Should We March?" (November 1942)

A. What double-victory campaign were African Americans waging at home and overseas? Why did Randolph believe that a March on Washington Movement was needed? What would a "nonviolent demonstration of Negro mass power" accomplish?

B. How do the points in Randolph's 1942 program build on his accomplishments in 1941 (Document 9)?

21. Franklin D. Roosevelt, Executive Order 9346 – Establishing a Committee on Fair Employment Practice (May 27, 1943)

A. What power to combat racial discrimination did EO 9346 give the Fair Employment Practices Committee? What potential problems would still remain? Why did EO 9346 also include language concerning labor unions?

B. How well did EO 9346 satisfy the demands of the March on Washington Movement (Document 20)?

22. United States Army Women's Auxiliary Corps, Questions and Answers About the WAAC (1943)

A. What tactics does this pamphlet use to entice women into joining the WAACs? How do the questions reveal the anxieties women might have about joining? Did the invitation to women to serve in uniform during the war upend gender roles?

B. How did serving in the WAACs compare to working for the war effort at home (Document 30)? Did men and women view female war work differently?

23. Ernie Pyle, "The Death of Captain Waskow" (January 10, 1944)

A. What emotions does Pyle's story convey? Pyle's story had to pass a censor; why would a military censor allow newspapers to publish this story?

B. How does Pyle's account of combat deaths compare to James Fahey's observations in his wartime diary (Document 19)?

24. Corporal Rupert Trimmingham's Letters to *Yank* Magazine (April 28, 1944 and July 28, 1944)

A. What incident prompted Trimmingham to write his first letter? Why did he write his second letter?

B. On what points would Trimmingham and A. Philip Randolph (Document 20) agree? How do their approaches to solving the problem of racial discrimination differ?

25. Dwight D. Eisenhower, D-Day Statement to the Allied Expeditionary Force (June 5 – 6, 1944)

A. What is Eisenhower's key message to troops before they attack? What different message does his second note convey? How do these documents influence your interpretation of the photo?

B. How do Eisenhower's two messages compare to the message that MacArthur issued in the Philippines (Document 28)?

26. Stopping the Holocaust (August 9 and August 14, 1944)

A. What differing opinions do Frischer and McCloy give on the question of bombing Auschwitz-Birkenau?

B. Which response to the Holocaust offered a stronger deterrent to genocide in time of war: the proposed bombing of Auschwitz-Birkenau or the postwar Nuremburg Trials (Document 34)?

Study Questions

27. Ansel Adams, Manzanar: Excerpt from *Born Free and Equal* (1944)

A. What do Adams' photographs of Manzanar reveal about the internment experience? How does Adams' text "instruct" readers on the meaning of his photographs? Why did he choose this title for his work? What was his purpose in publishing this book?

B. Compare the attitudes and actions of the Japanese-Americans in Adams' book with those of Toyosaburo Korematsu (Document 29). What are the differences and similarities?

28. General Douglas MacArthur, Radio Address Upon Returning to the Philippines (October 20, 1944)

A. What is the purpose of MacArthur's opening line? What is his message to the Filipino people?

B. How does MacArthur's view of the enemy compare to the description in James Fahey's *Pacific War Diary* (Document 19)?

29. *Korematsu v. US* (December 18, 1944)

A. What is the key argument of the majority opinion? What are the key arguments of the two dissenting opinions? What is the core of their disagreement?

B. What was the significance of wartime protests by Japanese Americans and African Americans (Documents 20 and 24) against violations of civil rights?

30. G. I. Roundtable Series, "Do You Want Your Wife to Work After the War?" (1944)

A. What are the key points made in defense of wives continuing to work after the war? What are the key points made against the wives continuing to work after the war?

B. This pamphlet purports to represent men's views on women working. Compare this pamphlet to the one recruiting women into the Women's Auxiliary Army Core (Document 22). What concerns do women have about joining the military? As presented by the pamphlets, do men and women share any concerns about women working outside of the home – and, if so, to what extent are their concerns similar?

31. Potsdam Declaration (July 26, 1945)

A. How does Truman's warning indirectly hint that the US has the atomic bomb? How did the Allies define the meaning of unconditional surrender for Japan? Which terms of surrender might Japan object to most? What incentives to surrender does the declaration give Japan?

B. How does this declaration apply the principles of the Atlantic Charter (Document 10) to the Pacific war?

32. Harry S. Truman, Press Release Alerting the Nation About the Atomic Bomb (August 6, 1945)

A. What points does Truman emphasize when explaining the development of the bomb? How does he justify its deployment? What does the existence of atomic bombs mean for the future?

B. Did the Potsdam Declaration (Document 31) adequately warn Japan of the risk of an atomic bomb attack?

33. United States Strategic Bombing Survey, *The Effects of Atomic Bombs on Hiroshima and Nagasaki* (July 1, 1946)

A. What assumptions does the report make about the future defense needs of the United States? What specific suggestions does it make about how best to defend the nation in a world with nuclear weapons?

B. How does this discussion of defending the United States compare to the discussions before Pearl Harbor over how best to defend the nation from attack (Documents 3, 4, 8, and 10)?

34. Justice Robert H. Jackson, *Report on the Nuremburg Trials* (October 7, 1946)

A. What are the key accomplishments of the trials, according to Jackson? What makes it an historic moment in international law?

B. In his opinion in *Korematsu v. US* (1944), Justice Hugo Black objected to applying the label "concentration camp" to the camps that detained Japanese Americans within the United States (Document 29). In what ways does Jackson's report on the Nuremburg Trials support or refute Justice Black's view?

Appendix C:
Suggestions For Further Reading

Adams, Michael C. C. *The Best War Ever: America and World War II*. Baltimore: Johns Hopkins University Press, 1994.

Blum, John Morton. *V Was for Victory: Politics and American Culture During World War II*. NY: Harcourt Brace Jovanovich, 1976.

The Bombing of Auschwitz: Should the Allies Have Attempted It? ed. Michael J. Neufeld and Michael Berenbaum. NY: St. Martin's Press, 2000.

Daniels, Roger. *Prisoners Without Trial: Japanese Americans in World War II*. NY: Hill and Wang, 2004.

Dower, John. *War Without Mercy: War and Power in the Pacific War*. NY: Pantheon Books, 1986.

Fussell, Paul. *Wartime: Understanding and Behavior in the Second World War*. NY: Oxford University Press, 1990.

Kennedy, David. *Freedom From Fear: The American People in Depression and War, 1929-1945*. NY: Oxford University Press, 1999.

Linderman, Gerald F. *The World Within War: America's Combat Experience in World War II*. Cambridge, MA: Harvard University Press, 1997.

Rosenberg, Emily. *A Date Which Will Live: Pearl Harbor in American Memory*. Durham, NC: Duke University Press, 2003.

Weinberg, Gerhard L. *A World at Arms: A Global History of World War II*. Cambridge: Cambridge University Press, 1994.

Permissions and Acknowledgments

Document 2, Bennett Champ Clark, "A Senator Defends the First Neutrality Act," originally published as "Detour Around War: A Proposal for a New American Policy," December 1935, *Harper's Monthly*, 1-9, © 1935 by Harper's Monthly. All rights reserved. Reprinted by permission [or insert appropriate lang.]

Document 7, "Eleanor Roosevelt Visits Tuskegee," originally published as Eleanor Roosevelt, "My Day, April 1, 1941," © 1941, by United Feature Syndicate, Inc. All rights reserved. Reprinted by permission of *The Eleanor Roosevelt Papers Digital Edition* (2017).

Document 8, Charles Lindbergh, "America First," originally published as *The text of Colonel Lindbergh's Address at a Rally of the America First Committee*, New York Times, *April 24, 1941*, © 1941 by Charles Lindbergh. All rights reserved. Reprinted by permission of Yale University.

Document 19, James J. Fahey, "Pacific War Diary," originally published as *Pacific War Diary, 1942-1945*, © 1963, and renewed 1991 by James J. Fahey. All rights reserved. Reprinted by permission of Houghton Mifflin Harcourt Publishing Company.

Document 23, Ernie Pyle, "The Death of Captain Waskow," originally distributed via Scripps-Howard wire, January 10, 1944, © 1944 by Ernie Pyle. All rights reserved. Reprinted by permission of the Scripps-Howard Foundation.

Document 26, "Stopping the Holocaust," reprinted courtesy of The Jacob Rader Marcus Center of the American Jewish Archives, Cincinnati, Ohio (americanjewisharchives.org).